Quaker Arrivals at Philadelphia

1682-1750

BEING A LIST OF CERTIFICATES OF REMOVAL
RECEIVED AT PHILADELPHIA MONTHLY
MEETING OF FRIENDS

BY

ALBERT COOK MYERS, M. L.

Southern Historical Press, Inc.
Greenville, South Carolina

Originally Published 1902

SOUTHERN HISTORICAL PRESS, INC.
PO BOX 1267
Greenville, SC   29601

ISBN #978-1-63914-062-6

Printed in the United States of America

INTRODUCTION

The following list of certificates of removal, now printed for the first time, will be of value, it is believed, not only to genealogists but to historians, in the broader sense, interested in investigating the early migratory movement to Penn's Colony.

As the metropolis of the new Province on the Delaware, Philadelphia became better known abroad than any other part of Pennsylvania, and a large proportion of the steady stream of Quaker colonists which poured into the Province made this city its objective point. Of the nineteen monthly meetings established in Pennsylvania prior to 1750, as the writer's investigation of the manuscript records has shown, Philadelphia Monthly Meeting easily ranks first as to the number of certificates received.

It is a significant fact that these Quaker immigrants to Philadelphia were among the most prominent and influential of that sect which, for the first three-quarters of a century of the existence of the Province, gave color to its social and political life, and remained the controlling force in governmental affairs.

Introduction

The Minutes of Burlington Monthly Meeting, in New Jersey, to which the Friends at Philadelphia belonged before the founding of their own monthly meeting, record that among the first meetings for Philadelphia Friends was that held at Thomas Fairman's house at Shackamaxon, now Kensington, in the early part of 1682. Later in the year, the meeting was removed to the city proper, and a meeting-house was erected. According to the Minutes of the Monthly Meeting, "The first Meeting of Friends of Philadelphia, to treat of business occurring among themselves, was held there the 9th day of the 11th month, being the third of the week, in the year 1682."

At this opening meeting steps were immediately taken that "friends of this meeting do bring in their Certificates from the respective meeting of friends they belong'd to in other Countries, and that they be Registred according to the time of their arrival here, in this province." At the next meeting, 12 Mo. 6, 1682, "Several friends brought in their Certificates as ordered by the foregoing meeting, but not being Endorsed with the time of their arrival were returned to them and Expected to be seen Endorsed the next meeting." At the following meeting, held 1 Mo. 6, 1683, "Certificates were brought in and Read. Agreed that they would be Registered and afterwards returned."

During the earliest years of the meeting's history nearly all the certificates of removal received were recorded, and but few of the originals were retained for preservation. Later, many of them were both recorded and preserved. A large number, however, were never recorded, and it was only recently that these unrecorded originals were arranged, mounted, and made accessible for examination.

In abstracting from the certificates, the writer has endeavored to include all the more important points of each certificate, and has quoted items that seemed especially interesting or quaint. When record of the receipt or arrival of a certificate has been found in the Minutes, it is noted. The early Minutes seldom record the receipt of a certificate, although the later Minutes do in most cases.

The compiler is especially grateful to George J. Scattergood, of Philadelphia, who kindly secured him access to the records at Fourth and Arch streets. He is also under obligations to William C. Cowperthwaite and Lydia

Introduction

Evans, of Friends' Book Store, at Fourth and Arch streets, for courtesies extended while he was examining the records. He is indebted to Joseph M. Truman, Jr., and Benjamin Walton, for permission to search the records at Fifteenth and Race streets; and he desires to thank Gilbert Cope, of West Chester, and Howard Williams Lloyd, of Germantown, for valued criticisms on the work.

ALBERT COOK MYERS.

Swarthmore College, Pennsylvania,
10 Mo. 10, 1900.

Certificates of Removal

ERRATA.

Introduction, p. iii, line 2, read "now printed for the first time *in book form.*"

p. 3, line 21, insert *Certificate* after *certain.*

p. 15, next to last line, *Mary,* not *Marry.*

p. 72, line 2, *Southwark,* not *Southwrack.*

CERTIFICATES OF REMOVAL RECEIVED AT PHILADELPHIA MONTHLY MEETING OF FRIENDS, 1682–1750.

"The first Meeting of Friends of Philadelphia, to treat of business occurring among themselves, was held there the 9th day of the 11th month, being the third day of the week, in the year 1682. . . . .
It is also agreed that the friends of this meeting do bring in their Certificates from the respective meeting of friends they belong'd to in other Countries, and that they be Registred according to the time of their arrival here, in this province."

At the meeting, 12 mo. 6, 1682, "Several friends brought in their Certificates as ordered by the foregoing meeting, but not being Endorsed with the time of arrival were returned to them and Expected to be seen Endorsed the next meeting." At the next meeting, held 1 mo. 6, 1682, "Certificates were brought in, and Read. Agreed that they should be Registred and afterwards returned." *

The list of certificates given below, including, after the year 1730, only foreign certificates, is compiled from the following records

---

* Minutes of Philadelphia Monthly Meeting.

of Philadelphia Monthly Meeting of Friends
or Quakers:

I. *The Original Book of Recorded Certificates Received*, in vault, at Friends' Meeting
House, Fifteenth and Race Streets, Philadelphia. An indexed copy is at the Library of
the Historical Society of Pennsylvania, Philadelphia.

II. *Men's Minutes* and *Women's Minutes* in
vault at Friends' Meeting House, Fourth and
Arch Streets, Philadelphia.

III. *Original Certificates*, many of which
are not recorded, lately arranged, mounted,
and indexed; in vault at Fourth and Arch
Streets.

RALPH FRETWELL, from Six Weeks Meeting, in Barbadoes Island, West Indies, he
"intending shortly to leave this Island."
Dated 12 mo. 11, 1683. The name of Thomas
ffretwell appears among the signers to the
certificate.

"Whereas it had been Reported by some
that Ralph Fretwell had in his hands the money
that hath been given by severall towards the
new Building of a Meeting House for ffriends
at the Bridge-Town : This is to Certify that
the said Matter was looked into by the last six
weeks Meeting of ffriends at Thomas Richards's
the tenth of this Instant, where it was made
Appear that ye sd. money was in Severall
Hands ; and none of it now (nor ever was)

in the Hands of the said Ralph : Witness our Hands the 20th—1st mo. 1683-4.''

JOHN JONES, from Plantation Meeting, Island of Barbadoes, desiring to remove with his family to Pennsylvania. Dated 5 mo. 15, 1683.

DAVID BRENTNALL, from Breach Meeting, Derbyshire, England, dated 8 mo. 10, 1681. Certificate addressed to '' ffriends at London or to whom it may concern.''

HENRY LEWIS, LEWIS DAVID, and WILLIAM HOWELL, from General Meeting at Redstone, in Pembrokeshire, South Wales, dated 6 mo. 6, 1682. Certificate was accepted by Philadelphia Monthly Meeting.

ROBERT ADAMS, from Barton Mo. Mtg. [England], dated 2 mo. 3, 1682. The name of Thomas Penn appears among signers.

JAMES ATKINSON, from Drogheda Meeting [Ireland], dated 8 mo. 23, 1681. At Phila. Mo. Mtg., 1 mo. 6, 1683, ''A certain, dated from Clanbrazill in the County of Armagh in Ireland, touching one James Atkinson (who now Resides at Griffith Jones's)'' was received.

SAMUEL ALLEN, from Monthly Meeting at Butcomb, Somersetshire, England, dated 12 mo. 24, 1681.

JANE BLANCHARD, from Mo. Mtg. at Ringwood, Hampshire, England, dated 11 mo. 11, 1682–3.

SAMUEL MILES, from Mo. Mtg. "in the Parish of Llainhangel yr hely gen," Radnorshire, Wales, dated 5 mo. 27, 1683.

WILLIAM FRAMPTON, from Half Year's Meeting at Oyster Bay, Long Island, dated 4 mo. 20, 1684.

ELIZABETH ANNIS, from Mo. Mtg. at Devonshire House, London, England, dated 5 mo. 5, 1682.

ALEXANDER BEARDSLEY. His certificate, read and accepted by Philadelphia Mo. Mtg., does not give either the date or the place whence he came, but the signers are as follows: Tho: Hackett, Wm: Pardoe, Tho: Reeves, John Knight, Job: Waring, Richard Parker, John Golbourn, Wm. Sankey, John Knight, "with several others."

ELIZABETH WALTER, certificate dated 7 mo. 13, 1683. Place not given, but signers were as follows: Peter Walter, Peter Walter, Jr., Christopher Holder, Jr., Richard Hill, "with several others."

WILLIAM SALWAY, from Mo. Mtg. at Taunton [England], dated 6 mo. 13, 1683.

JAMES MILES, from Mo. Mtg. "in the Parish of Llainhangell Helygen," Radnorshire. Wales, dated 5 mo. 27, 1683.

JOHN and RICHARD BUNCE, from Mo. Mtg. at "ffarrington" [England], dated 1 mo. 30, 1682.

THOMAS BOWMAN, from Meeting at Wansworth, county of Surrey, England, dated 2 mo. 4, 1682.

EVERARD BOULTON, from Mo. Mtg. at Rosse, in Herefordshire, England, dated 5 mo. 18, 1682.

BENJAMIN CHAMBERS, from Mo. Mtg. in City of Rochester, county of Kent, England, dated 5 mo. 18, 1682.

JOHN EVANS and DAVID KINSEY, from Bristol, England, dated 6 mo. 26, 1682.

THOMAS ELLIS, from Quarterly Meeting, at Dolyserre [Wales], dated 5 mo. 27, 1683.

PHILIP ENGLAND, from Men's Meeting, Dublin, Ireland, dated 3 mo. 21, 1683.

FRANCIS FINCHER, from Worcester England, dated 3 mo. 14, 1683.

ALEXANDER BEARDSLEY, JOHN PRICE, and SEE MERRY ADAMS, from Worcester, England, dated 3 mo. 14, 1683.

ENOCH FLOWER and JOSEPH BUSHELL, from Mo. Mtg. at Brinkworth [England], dated 3 mo. 21, 1683.

JOHN GARDNER and WILL: HARMER, from Mo. Mtg. at Purton, Wiltshire, dated 4 mo. 5, 1682. The name George Harmer appears among the signers.

JOHN GOODSON, from Mo. Mtg. at the Peel, in London, England, dated 6 mo. 30, 1682.

JOHN HART, from Mo. Mtg. at Witney, Oxfordshire, dated 2 mo. 10, 1682.

JOHN HARPER, from Mo. Mtg. at Barton [England], dated 2 mo. 3, 1682.

JOHN DAY and EDWARD JEFFERSON, from Ashwell Meeting [England], dated 3 mo. 12, 1682.

GILES KNIGHT, from Mo. Mtg. at Naylsworth [England], dated 2 mo. 11, 1682.

JOHN KILCOP, from Mo. Mtg. at Devonshire House, London, England, dated 5 mo. 12, 1682.

JOHN and JOSEPH LOW, from Men's Meeting at Bellyhagan, Parish of Kilmore, Ireland, dated 5 mo. 31, 1682.

CHARLES LEE, from Men's Meeting at Clithroe, Lancashire, England, dated 2 mo. 30, 1682.

JOHN MASON, from Mo. Mtg. at Farrington, county of Berks, England, dated 2 mo. 27, 1682.

ARCHIBALD MICHAEL, from Men's Meeting at Richard Boyes' House, near Lisburn, county of Antrim, Ireland, dated 6 mo. 2, 1682.

ELIZABETH NEWMAN, from Men's Meeting at Farrington [England], dated 1 mo. 30, 1682.

DAVID OGDEN, from London, England, dated 11 mo. 21, 1681–2.

EVAN OLIVER and DAVID JAMES, from Bristol, England, dated 6 mo. 26, 1682.

JOHN PARSONS and THO: KERELL. The certificate, dated 7 mo. 4, 1681, does not give place. The signers are: ''John Anderson, John Parsons & fflorence Parsons, his father and mother, Wm. Tyler, Joan Tyler, with many others.''

JAMES SESSIONS, from Mo. Mtg. at Witney [England], dated 5 mo. 10, 1682.

HANNAH SESSIONS, from Witney, dated 2 mo. 10, 1682.

THOMAS YONG, from Mo. Mtg. at Sangah, Yorkshire, England, dated 3 mo. 5, 1682.

MARY WOODARD, from Meeting at Devonshire House, London, England, dated 5 mo. 5, 1682.

HENRY WADDY. ''His Arrivall at Upland in Pennsilvania was the 2d Day of ye 6th mo. 1682.'' Place not mentioned.

RICHARD WORRALL, from Mo. Mtg. at Oare [England], dated 5 mo. 21, 1682.

RICHARD WALL, from Mo. Mtg. ''held at

ye House of Edward Edwards of Stock Orchard, in ye County of Glocester," England, dated 4 mo. 26, 1682.

JOHN WORRALL, from Meeting at Ore, Berkshire, England, dated 5 mo. 16, 1682.

THOMAS HOLME, from Meeting at Waterford City, Ireland, dated 11 mo. 29, 1681.

RICHARD WORRALL, from Mo. Mtg. at Ore, Berkshire, England, dated 1 mo. 17, 1682.

WILLIAM BRINTON. One certificate "which was given under the Hands of his Dealers & Correspondents," January 14, 1683, was subscribed by Thomas Brindley, John Clay, John Green, Josiah Stanney, with several others.
Another certificate, dated 11 mo. 15, 1683, from Mo. Mtg. at Dudley, [England]. Received 9 mo. 4, 1684.

GEORGE PYERCE [Pierce], from Mo. Mtg. at Frenshay, county of Glocester, England, dated 5 mo. 7, 1684. Another certificate from Thornbury Meeting. Received 9 mo. 4, 1684.

JOHN BOWTER, from Dudley Mo. Mtg, England, dated 3 mo. 21, 1684. Received 9 mo. 4, 1685.

JOHN TAYLOR and DANIEL OSBORN, from Kineton Meeting, Wiltshire, England, dated 5 mo. 13, 1684.

JOHN BANT and NICHOLAS PRIME. Place

not named. Certificate, dated 7 mo. 2, 1683, was signed by "Will: Bant & Tho: Bant ffather of ye said John, Thomas Lower, Tho: Salthouse, ffrancis ffox, with several others." Received 9 mo. 4, 1684.

JOHN TAYLOR. Certificate "being subcribed by the Parishioners of Aldrington in the County of Wilts [England], ye 17th of July, 1684, viyt. — Charles Gore, Esqr., Thomas Gore, Esqr., Isaac Osborn, Samson ffower, with several others." Received 9 mo. 4, 1684.

WILLIAM GARRET, JOHN SMITH, ROBERT CLIFFE, and SAMUEL LEWIS, from meeting at Harby, county of Leicester, England, dated 5 mo. 20, 1684. Received 9 mo. 4, 1684.

HUGH DURBOROW and JOSEPH HEMBEY [Hembray], from Somerset Ilchester, England, dated 6 mo. 6, 1684. Received 9 mo. 4, 1684.

DANIEL MEDLICOTT, from Mo. Mtg. at Salop, England, dated 2 mo. 16, 1683. At Phila., 9 mo. 4, 1684.

MARTHA SANKEY, from Salop, England, dated 3 mo. 13, 1683.

SAMUEL CARPENTER, from Mo. Mtg. at Bridge Town, Island of Barbadoes, dated 6 mo. 23, 1683.

HANNAH HARDYMAN, from Haverford West Meeting, England, dated, 6 mo. 2, 1683.

Among signers were Abraham Hardiman and Jane Hardiman, mother of Hannah. At Phila., 9 mo. 4, 1684.

Robert Turner and family, from Men's Meeting in the City of Dublin, dated 5 mo. 3, 1683. He being ''an Antient ffriend of this meeting'' and ''a Widdow man.''

Elizabeth Simms.—''Dear ffriends, These are, at ye Request of an old Servant of ours, Elizabeth Simms, to let you know that she hath Served us nine years and a half, where first she Received the visitation of ye blessed Truth, since which time she hath in generall behaved herself honestly and diligently, not without a sense of ye Truth and an operation of ye Power of it, which we earnestly desire she may mind, that she may approve herself a Blameless walker amongst you. She is clear of all Persons as to marriage that we can tell of, save one John Martin, and has been well Regarded of ffriends of ye meeting to which she has belonged. The Lord bless you and bless your Care for his Glory. Amen.

Your Reall ffriends in ye Truth,
WM. Penn,
Gulielma Maria Penn.''
Kensington, ye 2d 5 mo., 1685.

Sarah Hersent.
Rose Miller.

Michael and Elizabeth Hamond, from

Men's Meeting, in City of London, England, dated 6 mo. 25, 1686. Received 10 mo. 31, 1686.

MARY BULLOCKE, "Sometime of this Citty single women [Place not named], have aquainted yt she intends a voyage to Pensillvania and that ye Shipp she is now bound out on may suddenly depart before next men's meeting whereupon she have desired a Certificate on her behalf." Among signers were, John, William, Anne, and Grace Bullocke, Thomas Callowhill, etc.

WILLIAM BRADFORD and wife Elizabeth, from Devonshire House, London, England, dated 6 mo. 12, 1685. Among signers was Elizabeth Bradford. Received 11 mo. 4, 1685.

HANNAH SMITH, "ye Daughter of Robt. Smith an Honorable friend of our meeting formerly who deceased some years since." From Worcester City, England, dated 6 mo. 4, 1685.

WILLIAM FISHER, from Mo. Mtg. of Ross, county of Hereford, England, dated, 6 mo. 6, 1684. William and Samuel Fisher among signers.

JAMES CHICK, carpenter, unmarried, a member by convincement, from meeting at Callumpton, County of Devon, England, dated 12 mo. 25, 1683. The certificate was applied for at the meeting of Callumpton, 10 mo. 24, 1683, " by Richard Styling on ye behalf of one James Chick Carpenter (who was formerly his Servant and hath since Transported himself into Pennsilvania)."

SAMUEL RICHARDSON, wife and family, from Mo. Mtg. at Spanish Town, Island of Jamaica, dated 3 mo. 10, 1687.

FRANCIS GAMBLE, from Mo. Mtg. at " ye house of Thomas Richards," Barbadoes, dated 2 mo. 17, 1687. He "Having Intentions to goe of this Island to Pennsilvania for to Stay there some time, and to return hither again to his family wch thing he laid before our Monthly Meeting," 12 mo. 4, 1686. His wife is deceased. Received 6 mo. 26, 1687.

ELIZABETH CARTER, a single woman, who comes as a minister, from Spring Meeting, Barbadoes, dated 5 mo. 7, 1686.

THOMAS GODFREY, "of ye Town of Ashford, in ye County of Kent, Husbandman," and family; THOMAS BRIDGE, "of ye said Town of Ashford, being a single man;" THOMAS HEANAKER, "of Woodchurch, in ye Said County, Sonn in Law to ye said Tho: Godfrey." All in one certificate from meeting at Mersham, England, dated 7 mo. 9, 1686. Among signers are Thomas Brett, of Mersham, and Thomas Brett, of Bonnington.

FRANCIS COOKE, unmarried, of Little

Hallum, County of Darby, England, "is gone for Pennsylvania." From Mo. Mtg. at Breach House, county of Darby, England, dated 5 mo. 13, 1682.

MARY BRETT, widow of John Brett, of Mershan, and son Daniel, from Mo. Mtg. at Mershan, county of Kent, England, dated 7 mo. 8, 1687. "We lately come to understand" that they "was arrived amongst you at Phylad," in safety. She was an inhabitant in Mershan "diver years." Among signers were Thomas, Mary, and Elizabeth Brett.

ALEXANDER BEARDSLEY, wife and family. Date and place not mentioned. Signers: Edward Bourne, Thomas Reeves, John Golbourn, Richard Parker, William Pardoe, Joseph Allibon, William Sankey, Edward Stanton, James Taylor, Thomas Hackett, John Hunt, Thomas Mince, and John Knight.

JAMES MARSHALL, wife Rachel, and family, and WILLIAM HUDSON, unmarried, "ye younger," all of York City, England. Certificate from Mo. Mtg. in York. No date. Among signers was Wm. Hudson.

JAN WILLIAMS BOOKENHOVEN, "a Cooper who having lately lived at Haarlem, and now with his Wife and Children Intending for Pensilvania hath desired of this meeting an Attestation to shew unto you." From Mo. Mtg. in Amsterdam, Holland, dated 5 mo. 3, 1684.

[John Williamson Bockenhoven was Sophia Armitt's father.]

"And dear Brethren as for you the Eyes of many nations are turned towards you in expectation whether your governmt & making of lawes & also ye execution of ye same will agree with the Testimonies of the faithfull Servants of ye Lord, in this age whose Pfession concerning those Pticulars formerly hath bin published to the World."

SARAH WATTS, dated 11 mo. 27, 1686, from Radnor Mo. Mtg., Pa. Not recorded.

EDWARD TURNER, dated 1 mo. 14, 1686–7, from Concord Mo. Mtg., Pa. To marry Catharine Carter. Not recorded. At Phila., 12 mo. 25, 1686–7.

GEORGE SMEDLEY, unmarried, dated 4 mo. 15, 1687, from Darby Mo. Mtg., Pa. Not recorded. At Phila., 3 mo. 27, 1687. Married Sarah Gooden.

SEEMERRIE ADAMS, in order to marry Mary Britt, widow, of Philadelphia. Dated 8 mo. 5, 1687, from Falls Mo. Mtg., Bucks Co., Pa. Not recorded. At Phila., 7 mo. 30, 1687.

FRANCIS COOKE, unmarried, of Blackbird Creek, New Castle county, dated 4 mo. 19, 1687, from Duck Creek. Not recorded. At Phila., 3 mo. 27, 1687.

WILLIAM BETHELL, unmarried, of Amboyperth, New Jersey, Bricklayer, "hath for the space of three years & an half lived in the said place.'' Dated 7 mo. 14, 1687, from Mo. Mtg. at Amboy Perth. To marry Eleanor Claypoole. Not recorded. At Phila. 10 mo. 30, 1687.

JOSHUA TITTERY, to marry Cicely Wolley; dated 1 mo. 26, 1688, from Abington Mo. Mtg., Pa. Not recorded. At Phila., 12 mo. 24, 1687.

JOHN McCOMB, unmarried, dated 6 mo. 19, 1688, from William Stockdale. Not recorded. At Phila., 5 mo. 26, 1688.

WILLIAM SALWAY, to marry Sarah Pennock, dau. of Christopher, of Phila., dated 6 mo. 22, 1688, from Abington Mo. Mtg. Not recorded.

JOHN BARNES, Tailor, in order to marry Mary Arnell, dated 7 mo. 24, 1688, from Abington Mo. Mtg., Pa. Not recorded.

THOMAS CARLE, to marry Catharine Brintnall, dated 8 mo. 3, 1688, from Falls Mo. Mtg., Pa. Not recorded.

WILLIAM RODNEY, unmarried, dated 10 mo. 18, 1688, from Sarah Edmondson and William Pavatt, of Talbot Co., Md. Also a certificate dated 10 mo. 18, 1688, signed in behalf of the quarterly meeting by William Dixon. Not recorded. Declared intentions of marriage with Marry Hollyman, at Phila., 9 mo. 30, 1688.

JAMES STANFIELD, son of Francis and Grace, to marry Mary Hutchinson, daughter of George, of Burlington, dated 12 mo. 3, 1689–90, from Chester Mo. Mtg., Pa. Not recorded. At Phila., 3 mo. 30, 1690.

WILLIAM SAY, sawyer, of Burlington; to marry Mary, daughter of Widow Guest; dated 8 mo. 5, 1690, from Burlington Mo. Mtg., New Jersey. At Phila., 8 mo. 31, 1690. Not recorded.

THOMAS TURNER, on a religious visit, dated 7 mo. 24, 1697, from Quarterly Mtg. of Coxall, Essex, England. Received 5 mo. 28, 1704. Not recorded.

JOHN LYNDHAM, "of Ann Arundel County in Province of Maryland, came to a monthly meeting held at ye house of Wm: Richardson at West River, the 20th 9 mo., 1691, and Laid before ye meeting his Intention of Removeing to dwell at Pennsilvania." Dated 9 mo. 22, 1691.

MARGARET LINEHAM, from Mo. Mtg. at West River, Maryland, dated 11 mo. 15, 1691.

RALPH JACKSON, from Mo. Mtg. held at West River, Maryland, 5 mo. 1, 1692. Received 5 mo. 29, 1692.

GEORGE GRAY, widower, "an Ancient inhabitant of this Island," intending to visit and do business in Pennsylvania, from Quarterly Meeting "at ye House of Richard Sutton,"

Barbadoes Island.   Dated 1 mo. 24, 1691–2.
Received 5 mo. 29, 1692.

EVAN MORRIS, wife Gainor, and two children, "wch are and hath bin faithfull to ye Testimony in ye time of theire Suffring & Imprisonmt: and always Since they were Convinced of ye Truth they walked accordingly." "Also for some years past having his mind inclind for Pensilvania." From "Quarterly Meeting at Tyddyn y Garreg for ye County of Merioneth," Wales, dated 5 mo. 8, 1690.

THOMAS GRIFFITH, unmarried, of Westchester, England.   Certificate from Chester, England, dated 6 mo. 9, 1686.

BARBARA PRACHIN, "Relict of Hillarius Prachin," MARIANA VAN BUYLAERT, "Relict of Jno. Van Buylaert," and ABIGAIL MATERN, "ye Daughter of John George Matern, School Master, Deceased." The women "(mother, daughter & Grandaughter)" are free in relation to marriage.   Certificate from Two Weeks' Meeting, in London, England, dated 12 mo. 5, 1693–4.

PENTICOST TEAG and wife, "he being Capable of ye Trade or Occupation of ffishery," from Mo. Mtg. at Marazion, in Cornwall, England, dated 1 mo. 5, 1693–4; also endorsed at Fallmouth, 1 mo. 7, 1693–4. Received 5 mo. 27, 1694.

JOSEPH WHITE, "have Removed himself

with his wife and Children," to Pennsylvania. Certificate from New Salem, dated 5 mo. 30, 1694.

REBECCA RICHARDSON, young woman, "yt some of us have known her from her Youth." Certificate dated 2 mo. 4, 1681, is addressed to Friends in New York or any other place. Place is not named. Signers: Mary Stott, Ann Whitehead, Grace Bathurst, Mary Plumsted, Mary Ellson, Mary Morden, ffra: Polsted, Pris: Hart, Margt. Meakins, Marabella ffarmbrow.

STEPHEN COLEMAN and wife, from Half Year's Meeting, at Chester, Kent Co., Md., dated 2 mo. 12, 1697.

RICHARD HOSKINS, minister, wife and family, from Quarterly Meeting at "ye house of Thomas Pilgrim," Barbadoes, dated 7 mo. 24, 1696. He had traveled "much for ye propogation" of truths "in Severall Countries."

NATHANIEL HARDING, "Cittizen and Skinner of London," wife and family. Certificate from Mo. Mtg. at Devonshire House, London, England, dated 10 mo. 11, 1695.

ELIZABETH WEBB, minister, of Gloucester, England, on a religious visit to America. Certificate from Quarterly Mtg. at Tetbury, county of Gloucester, England, dated 6 mo. 31, 1697. Richard Webb was a signer.

MARY ROGERS, minister, wife of Joseph Rogers, "of the Towne of East Markham, in this County of Notingham." She asked for a certificate 7 mo. 27 [year not given], "at our Quarterly Meeting In Mansfeild," England.

RICHARD WARDER, "Some Small tyme was a member of this meeting," and now intends to remove with wife and family to Pennsylvania ; from Mo. Mtg. at Arundell, England, dated 4 mo. 7, 1698.

JOHN BUSBY, weaver, of Milton, in the Parish of Shipton, "and belonging to the Meeting at Milton." Certificate dated 2 mo. 4, 1682.

EVAN POWELL, weaver, and wife Gwen, of Nantmell, Radnorshire, Wales, dated 3 mo. 20, 1698.

EDWARD MOORE, widower, "of the Psh. of Lanbudaen," Radnorshire, Wales, with his family, and neighbor, THOMAS POWELL, dated 3 mo. 20, 1698.

JOHN ASKEW, unmarried, heretofore servant to John Bellers, of Peters Chalfont, "county of Bucks, England," having formerly lived sometime ["about two years"] in this County * * * did some tyme since transport himself into Pensilvania," and now desires a certificate. Certificate from Mo. Mtg. at Hunger Hill, for the upper side of the County of Bucks, England, dated 1 mo. 1, 1695.

JOHN BYE, unmarried, son of Thomas Bye, "a member of our monthly meeting haveing some tyme Since Lived with his father but now is Resident ·in your parts," of Pennsylvania, desires a certificate. From Mo. Mtg. at Horsleydowne, in Southwark, England, dated 6 mo. 3, 1698.

LUMLY WILLIAMS, unmarried, "of the towne of Radnor intends to goe to pensilvania." Certificate from Meeting in Radnorshire, Wales, dated 3 mo. 20, 1698.

RICHARD LOW, unmarried, "late of black fryers in London Shooemaker proposes unto us his Intentions of transporting himself into pensilvania." From Mo. Mtg. of Bull and Mouth, City of London, England, dated 3 mo. 10, 1682.

ELIZABETH JANNEY, unmarried, from Mo. Mtg. at "Monley" [Morley], Cheshire, England; dated 2 mo. 6, 1698. Name of Randle Janney among signers.

WILLIAM MANINGTON, unmarried, having his father's consent, desires a certificate. From Mo. Mtg. at Gloucester City, England, dated 2 mo. 30, 1699. Among signers are Thomas Manington and William Manington.

WILLIAM WILSON, "our Ancient and well beloved friend * * * with his son John Wil son & famyly hath reported to us their Intention of transporting themselves over the Seas

In order to Setle. * * * our friend William Wilson was Anciently Convinced of the truth & did bear ye burden In ye heat of the day both by Imprisonment and spoiling of goods. * * * And his son John Wilson hath been Educated to follow his fathers Steps in ye truth butt have not been soe well guided as wee Could have wished butt was drawne Aside by vaine Company notwthstanding the Advice of friends to ye Contrary butt of late he was visited with a sore fitt of sickness In all apearance nott likely to live In wch wee doe believe he saw himself as he was seen and repented * * * he is a good workman a Carpenter by trade and fitt to take work in hand. And his wife was borne & Convinced amongst us and hath been of a sober behaviour." From Mo. Mtg. at Woodhall, in Calbeck, county of Cumberland, England, dated 9 mo. 16, 1699.

VINCENT CALDWELL, unmarried, from Mo. Mtg. at Moniash, England, dated 1 mo. 24, 1699.

WILLIAM PENN, from Two Days' Meeting, by appointment, at London, England, dated 6 mo. 11, 1699. "These are to accompany our deare and Esteemed ffriend Willm: Penn whom wee honour in the Lord and prefer in love as he is worthy for the works sake wch god has made him Instrumentall in to his truth and Chosen people who holding fast the faithful word whereby he has been able by sound Doctrine both to Exhort and to Convince the gain Sayers of whose Service on this account there are Clouds of witnesses: god having been pleased allsoe to Endow wth wisdom and hath given him Interest in the hearts of princes and our Rulers Even in tyme of Sore persecution and great Suferings * * * ''

''This last 2d day was our monthly meetting of ministering friends where this our deare ffriend William Penn was present and tooke the leave of the brethren * * * the lord helpe him in all things and by his good providence bring him back again to his native Country * * * ''

''*postscript.*

Our deare friends Thos: Turner, Will: Ellis and Walter fossett of our Country and Tho. Chalkly are all Safly Arrived some tyme since and Eliz: Web: lately: and now are with us two of the brethren from yon vizt Richard Hoskius and Joseph Kirkbride, by these our friends wee have Receved Epistles and letters from you wch as well as themselves, have given us good accounts of ye prosperity of truth in ye provinces beyond the seas wch is our Comfort to heare: the lord prosper yett more and more among you. farewell.''

WILLIAM PENN, another certificate, from Meeting in the City of Bristol, England, dated 5 mo. 31, 1699, where ''of late he hath had his residence some tyme.'' Another from Mo.

Mtg. held at Horsham, England, dated 5 mo. 12, 1699.

SARAH CLEMENS, minister, certificate to make a religious visit, from Mo. Mtg. at Devonshire House, London, England, dated 6 mo. 9, 1699.

THOMAS WILSON and family, from Mo. Mtg. at Lancaster, England, dated 1 mo. 11, 1699.

THOMAS PEARSON, wife Grace, and children, from Marsden Meeting, Lancashire, England, dated 12 mo. 16, 1698.

THOMAS LOYNSDALL [Lansdale] and wife, from Mo. Mtg. at Lancaster, dated 1 mo. 11, 1698–9.

JONATHAN DINNIS, "of this Island Surveyor haveing lately been much troubled with Consumpton," desires to take a voyage to Pennsylvania for his health, leaving behind his wife and children. Certificate from Plantation Meeting, Barbadoes, dated 7 mo. 22, 1699.

JOHN WARDER, unmarried, from Mo. Mtg. at Horsleydowne, Southwark, England, dated 6 mo. 2, 1699. Received 10 mo. 29, 1699.

THOMAS BYE (and son), whom "we have known * * * above twenty years," desires to go to Pennsylvania to be followed later by wife and family. From Mo. Mtg. at Horsleydowne, in Southwark, England, dated 5 mo. 5, 1699. Received 10 mo. 24, 1799.

SOLOMON WARDER and MARY HOWEL, from First Day Meeting on Newport, Isle of Wight, dated 6 mo. 20, 1699. They declared their intentions of marriage at the Mo. Mtg. held 6 mo. 2, 1699, and no obstructions appeared. "But the Speedy departure of the Ship has hindered their appearing att our next Monthly Meeting for the Accomplishment of their said Intention." Received 10 mo. 29, 1699.

THOMAS PARSON, "Seigr of Coufold," county of Sussex, single man, who has suffered for the truth. From Mo. Mtg. at Horsham, in Sussex, England, dated 5 mo. 12, 1699. Names of Hugh and Isaac Parson among signers. Received 10 mo. 29, 1699.

RANDOLPH JANNEY, son of William Janney, of Hanford, Cheshire, England. From Mo. Mtg. at Morley, Cheshire, England, dated 6 mo. 2, 1699. Name of Deborah Janney among signers. Received 10 mo. 29, 1699.

JAMES STREATER, of New Alsford, and family, from Mo. Mtg. in Alton, Hampshire, England, dated 6 mo. 4, 1699. Received 10 mo. 29, 1699.

TIMOTHY HUDSON, young, single man, son of William Hudson, from Mo. Mtg. at York, England, dated 11 mo. 6, 1698-9. Has consent of parents. Received 11 mo. 26, 1699.

JOSEPH AUSTILL, "lately of Ore," son of

William Austill, and grandson of Dorothy Austill, deceased, "an honorable woman in the truth." From Meetings of Ore and Newberry, England, dated 11 mo. 17, 1698–9. Received 11 mo. 26, 1699.

WILLIAM SMITH, "the Elder," wife and family, from Mo. Mtg. at Glastenbury, Somersetshire, England, dated 6 mo. 14, 1699.

SAMUEL SIDON, who "did much good by Administring physich." From Meeting at Breach, Derbyshire, England, dated 7 mo. 22, 1699.

ABRAHAM SCOTT, "of Bartholomew ye great Mercer son of thomas Scott of ye same place and trade, deceased." From Mo. Mtg. at Peale, in St. John Street, London, England, dated 5 mo. 26, 1699. Received 11 mo. 26, 1699.

THOMAS STOREY ("abode wth us about nine months") from Mo. Mtg. at Hamersmith, county of Middlesex, England, dated 5 mo. 27, 1699. Received 11 mo. 26, 1699.

JAMES BARTON, unmarried, "baker lately dwelling wth in the Compass of the Peele meetting In St. Johns Street soe Called Son of James Barton of Uti & ster in the County of Staford, farmer." From Two Weeks' Meeting at Devonshire House, London, dated 2 mo. 10, 1699. Received 11 mo. 26, 1699.

JONATHAN DICKINSON ("now a Resident

amongst us"), from Mo. Mtg. at Spanish Town, Island of Jamaica, dated 1 mo. 12, 1699.

JOHN LINTON, and wife, Rebecca, late of Wigton. From Mo. Mtg. at Long Newton, England, dated 6 mo. 25, 1699. He "walked amongst us these severall yeares." "She Came of beleveing parents and was Educated in ye way of truth from Childhood."

MARY DOE, unmarried, late servant to John Field, from Mtg. at Brewers Hall, London, England; dated 5 mo. 17, 1699. Not recorded.

JOAN HALL, unmarried, dated 11 mo. 4, 1699, from Mo. Mtg. at Moniash, Derbyshire, England. Signed by Sarah Hall. Not recorded.

ROBERT HEATON, to marry Grace Pearson, dated 2 mo. 4, 1700, from Middletown Mo. Mtg., Bucks Co., Pa.; at Phila., 1 mo. 29, 1700. Not recorded.

THOMAS ENGLAND, unmarried, dated 3 mo. 27, 1700, from Chester Mo. Mtg., Pa. At Phila., 3 mo. 31, 1700. Not recorded.

SAMUEL HOOD, son of John Hood, to marry —— Hudson, of Philadelphia; dated 12 mo. 5, 1700, from Darby Mo. Mtg., Pa. At Phila., 12 mo. 28, 1700. Not recorded.

THOMAS TAYLOR, to marry Rachel Minshall, of Philadelphia; dated 8 mo. 28, 1700, from

Chester Mo. Mtg., Pa. Received 9 mo. 29, 1700. Not recorded.

JOSEPH HOOD, son of John Hood, to marry Sarah Brown, of Philadelphia. Dated 12 mo. 5, 1700, from Darby Mo. Mtg., Pa. Received 12 mo. 28, 1700. Not recorded.

HENRY WILLIS, "Antient," from Flushing, dated 3 mo. 26, 1700.

RICHARD HILL, JR., mariner, unmarried, from Two Weeks' Meeting, London, England, dated 6 mo. 14, 1699. Certificate addressed to Mo. Mtg. at West River, Maryland, or elsewhere. He had obtained a certificate from Mo. Mtg. at West River, Md., dated 2 mo. 29, 1698 (?) and presented to Friends in London. Received 6 mo. 30, 1700.

JOHN HURFORD, "late of Teverton, in the County of Devon," England, and family. Also "yt John Hurford, Jur., his son, and July an Holcomb his own wife's daughter," are free in relation to marriage. From Meeting at Columpton, dated 2 mo. 24, 1700.

RICHARD PARKER, from Bristol, England, received 2 mo. 25, 1701.

JOHN WEBB and family, of the City of Gloucester, England, from Quarterly Mtg. of Co. of Gloucester, at Nailsworth, dated 6 mo. 27, 1700. Received 11 mo. 31, 1700.

MARY LAWSON, unmarried, from Mo. Mtg. upon Pardsay Crag, held 6 mo. 27, 1700.

She was convinced "about three yeares agoe." Received 11 mo. 31, 1700.

WILLIAM ABBOTT and daughter, from Bandon Mo. Mtg., Ireland; received 2 mo. 25, 1701.

HANNAH EMERSON, unmarried, from Mtg. at Cockermouth, Cumberland, England, dated 11 mo. 17, 1697. She "hath lived near us Since she was a Child, and for Sometime lately hath lived wthin the Compas of our meeting." Received 11 mo. 31, 1700.

NICHOLAS FAIRLAMB, "hath lived and belonged to our meetting the time of his Aprentisship and Since he hath been loose from his Mr: being seaven years hath behaved himselfe orderly and honestly." From Mo. Mtg. at Stockton, Co. of Durham, England, dated 6 mo. 13, 1700. Received 9 mo. 29, 1700.

JOHN GIBBINS, JR., of Bethell, Chester Co., Pa.; certificate to Phila. from Concord Mo. Mtg., Chester Co., dated 7 mo. 9, 1700. Intending to marry Sarah Howard, of Phila. Under date of 7 mo. 24, 1700, from Bethell, John and Margery Gibbins gave consent to the marriage of their son, John, to Sarah Howard.

TOBIAS DIMOCK, unmarried, from Town of Newport, Rhode Island, dated 10 mo. 12, 1699. He "hath for about four year last past resided amongst us." Received 7 mo. 27, 1700.

JOHN LEA and family, of the City of Gloucester, England, from Quarterly Meeting held at Naylsworth, County of Gloucester, dated 6 mo. 27, 1700. Received 11 mo. 31, 1700.

HUGH CORDRY and family, from Mo. Mtg. at Rattclife, near London, England, dated 10 mo. 27, 1699.

DEBORAH CORDRY, "to remove from hence in order to go unto her husband Hugh Cordry at Pensilvania." Dated 10 mo. 27, 1700, from Mo. Mtg. at Ratclif, England.

JOSEPH ANTROBUS, unmarried, son of Benjamin Antrobus, of London. From Two Weeks' Mtg. in London, England, dated 3 mo. 6, 1700.

JOHN WALKER, a young man, unmarried, who "has for Some tyme Resided in Philadelphia yt went out of Maryland." From Mo. Mtg. in Maryland, dated 3 mo. 30, 1700. Received 9 mo. 29, 1700.

WILLIAM and ROSAMOND TILL, "Son and Daughter of John Till: of Whitegreave, a member of our Meeting." They are going in "Care of our friends Robrt Heath & his wife who Come along ye Same voyage wth them & allsoe to Ann Delworth an Inhabitant of your Country." From Stafford Mo. Mtg., England, dated 2 mo. 11, 1700. Among signers is John Till, "their father."

GEORGE ARCHERS, a certificate concerning him from the Mo. Mtg. in the county of Somerset, England, was read at Philadelphia Mo. Mtg., 7 mo. 27, 1700, "giving an account of his being disowned by friends."

BENJAMIN DAVIS, unmarried, from Mtg. held at ffrench hay, Co. of Gloucester, England, dated 3 mo. 6, 1695. Received 9 mo. 29, 1700.

RACHEL MINSHALL, from Preparative Mtg. at Frandly, Cheshire, England, dated 1 mo. 3, 1697.

THOMAS CHALKLY and wife, Martha, from Mo. Mtg. at Horsleydowne, Southwark, England, dated 6 mo. 28, 1700. Among signers were: George Chalkly, Sgr. and George Chalkly, Jr.

ANNA WATSON, unmarried, from Quarterly Mtg. at the Bull and Mouth, London, England, dated 8 mo. 6, 1701.

JOHN ESTAUGH, Minister, of Dunmore, Co. of Essex. Has visited England and Holland. From Quarterly Mtg. at Cogshall, Co. of Essex, England, dated 7 mo. 28, 1700. Received 1 mo. 27, 1702.

CHRISTOPHER BLACKBURNE, from Mo. Mtg. of Richmond, held at Leburn, Co. of York, England, dated 12 mo. 13, 1701. Now in Pennsylvania; having lost first certificate, desired another. He was at Phila. Mo. Mtg. 4 mo. 26, 1702.

JAMES STEEL, of Chichester, Co. of Sussex, a house carpenter, wife and family, from Mo. Mtg. at Steyning, Sussex, dated 5 mo. 6, 1702. Among signers are: Henry Steell and John Hammond (father of James Steel's wife).

LEVIN HERBERDINK, an aged Friend "who dwelled there many years in ye Germantownship being resolved to leave his Plantation, & the harder work attending ye same, hath removed himself & family to the City of Philadelphia, in good hopes to live a more comfortable life." From Mo. Mtg. of Dublin Twp. [Abington, Phila. Co.], "att ye house of Richard Worrell," dated 12 mo. 22, 1702–3.

WILLIAM ROBINSON, a young man, unmarried, of Rounton, from Mo. Mtg. at Thirsk, Yorkshire, England, dated 10 mo. 8, 1702. Among signers are: Jo. Robinson, Samuel Robinson, Tho. Robinson and Nich. Robinson. Original Certificate. Received 2 mo. 30, 1703.

JOSEPH PARKER, a young lad. Elizabeth Parker, of Bartholomew Close, London, England, widow, desires a certificate for her son Joseph Parker, "a Lad of fourteen years of age" who is going "over to an Uncle of his (viz:) Robert Heath," in Pennsylvania. From Mo. Mtg. at the Peel, London, dated 12 mo. 25, 1701. Received 2 mo. 30, 1703.

BENJAMIN CHANDLEE, unmarried, son of William Chandlee, of Kilmore, Co. of Kildare,

Ireland.   From Edenderry Mtg., King's Co., Ireland, dated 11 mo. 28 [year not given]. Some of signers: Wm. Chandlee, Jr. and Nath. Chandlee.

MARGARET BYE and two daughters, certificate from Horsleydown Mtg., England, received 4 mo. 27, 1701.

JOHN PICKOTT, or Piggott, unmarried, "who some time resided amongst us here & lately removing himself into Philadelphia," desires a certificate.   From Mo. Mtg. at West River, Maryland, dated 11 mo. 29, 1702-3. Marriage to Alice Renier authorized 8 mo. 27, 1704.

ELIZABETH GREEN, unmarried, "lived here in this City several years." From Mtg. at Dublin, Ireland, dated 11 mo. 26, 1702. Received 4 mo. 25, 1703.

ROBERT FINLEY, "who hath been a Captive in Barbary Nineteen years and convinced there Sixteen years before he was redeemed from thence by friends.   Hath since his redemption mostly had his Residence when in England in & about this City." Unmarried. From Two Weeks' Mtg. at Bull and Mouth, London, England, dated 1 mo. 22, 1702-3. Received 6 mo. 27, 1703.

RACHEL CUMBERLIDGE, from London, England, received 4 mo. 26, 1702.

SAMUEL HELD [Heald] and wife Mary,

both born of believing parents, from Mo. Mtg. held at Morley, Co. of Chester, England, dated 10 mo. 3, 1702. Joan Held, a signer. Received 5 mo. 30, 1703.

THOMAS IREDELL, a young man, unmarried, from Mo. Mtg. at Pardsay Cragg, in Cumberland, England, dated 6 mo. 27, 1700. Received 8 mo. 29, 1703.

RICHARD ROBINSON, unmarried, leather dresser, "hath been a Captive in barbary four years and convinced of truth thear about fourteen months before he was redeemed thence by friends: and since his Redemption when in England had his Residence in and about this City." From Two Weeks' Mtg. at Bull and Mouth, London, England, dated 1 mo. 22, 1702–3. Received 9 mo. 26, 1703.

RICHARD WEBB, of City of Gloucester, England, and family, from Quarterly Mtg. at Naylsworth, County of Gloucester, England, dated 6 mo. 27, 1700. Original certificate. Received 12 mo. 28, 1700.

PETER STRETCH, wife and family, from Mo. Mtg. at Leek, Staffordshire, England, dated 10 mo. 3, 1702. Received 6 mo. 27, 1703.

MARGERY KEITH, unmarried, from Bridgetown Mo. Mtg., Barbadoes, dated 3 mo. 28, 1702. John Beek, at our last Mo. Mtg., desired a certificate for his *sister* Margery Keith

("who hath Lately made profession of Truth.")
Also another certificate from same meeting
dated 8 mo. 29, 1702, in which, John Beeke,
"belonging to ye bridge meeting Desired a
certificate for his Sister in Law Margery Keith
Lately gone hence to pensilvania."

JOAN CLIFTON, "being Lately Removed
from this Side to Philadelphia." From Mo.
Mtg. held at Newtown, West New Jersey,
dated 4 mo. 8, 1704. Received 5 mo. 28,
1704.

MICHAEL WALTON, unmarried, of Stockton,
from Mtg. at Norton, Co. of Durham, England, dated 4 mo. 10, 1684.

NATHAN FAUCETT, unmarried, from Mo.
Mtg. held at Providence [Chester Mo. Mtg.],
Co. of Chester, Pa., dated 9 mo. 27, 1704.
John Fawsitt a signer. At Phila., 9 mo. 24,
1704.

HANNAH SCOTT, unmarried, from Mo. Mtg.
at Burlington, New Jersey, dated 5 mo. 3,
1704.

CHRISTOPHER TOPHAM, unmarried, of Cold-
ban, in the Parish of Cornham, Co. of York,
England, Shoemaker. From Richmond Mo.
Mtg. held at Leyborn, Co. of York, dated 6
mo. 13, 1703. Received 10 mo. 29, 1704.

THOMAS COLEMAN, unmarried, from Mo.
Mtg. at Horsleydown, in Southwark, England,

dated 1 mo. 8, 1703–4. Original preserved. Received 11 mo. 26, 1704.

WILLIAM PETTY, wife Jane and family. Some of children married to those "not strictly in the profession of truth." They came from Norwich, England, to New Jersey. From Mo. Mtg. held at Burlington, New Jersey, dated 7 mo. 4, 1704. Received 8 mo. 27, 1704.

ANN VEERE, spinster, proposed her intention of removal to Penna. at Mo. Mtg. for Westminster held at the Savoy, London, 12 mo. 3, 1702. From Two Weeks' Mtg. in London, England, dated 12 mo. 8, 1702.

KATHARINE HALLINGAM, unmarried, being removed to settle in Phila. From Mo. Mtg. at Newtown, West Jersey, dated, 2 mo. 12, 1705.

THOMAS COLEMAN, dated 6 mo. 23, 1704, from Horslydown, England. He was in haste to take the ship which "was fallen Down the River, in order to her Voyage." Dated 6 mo. 23, 1704, from Mo. Mtg. at Horslydown, in Southwark, England. Received 11 mo. 26, 1704.

ABIGAIL HOOD, widow, with children, dated 7 mo. 6, 1704, from Mo. Mtg. at Darby, Pa. At Phila., 12 mo. 23, 1704. Not recorded.

DAVID WILLIAM, widower, to marry Mary Malsby, of Phila., dated 11 mo. 11, 1704, from Haverford Mo. Mtg., Pa. At Phila., 10 mo, 29, 1704. Not recorded.

ANN CHOPMAN, of Wrightstown, to make a religious visit to Long Island and Rhode Island; dated 1 mo. 1, 1704–5, from Middletown Mo. Mtg., Bucks Co., Pa. Not recorded.

JEDIAH HUSSEY, in order to marry; dated 6 mo. 4, 1705, from Newark or Kennett Mo. Mtg. Received 6 mo. 31, 1705. Not recorded.

MARY NEWCOME, of Lockington, Co. of Leicester, a Minister, to make a religious visit; dated 1 mo. 28, 1706, from Leicester Quarterly Meeting, England. Not recorded.

SAMUEL LEWIS, to marry Grissell Kite; dated 11 mo. 2, 1706, from Haverford Mo. Mtg., Pa. At Phila., 8 mo. 28, 1709. Not recorded.

ABRAHAM SCOTT, unmarried, "who Lately Transported himself from your province to this citty, the place of his former Residence, and also brought with him a Certificate" from you. From Two Weeks' Mtg. in London, England, dated 11 mo. 12, 1701. Received 3 mo. 26, 1705.

THOMAS LYFORD, unmarried, from Two Weeks' Mtg. at Bull and Mouth, in London, England, dated 11 mo. 22, 1704. He had produced a certificate to London from Phila., of date 2 mo. 28, 1704. Received 4 mo. 29, 1705.

JOHN WIDOWFEILD, a young man, "who has been Conversant amongst a few years also Since he came Among friends." From Mo. Mtg. at Thirske, Yorkshire, England, dated 7 mo. 14, 1703. Also a letter to John Widdowfield from Mo. Mtg. at Thirk, dated 4 mo. 12, 1705, certifying that said Widdowfield was unmarried when he left England. Original preserved. Received 4 mo. 29, 1705.

ELIZABETH and ELINOR ARNOLD, unmarried, "was brought up by William Browne an honest friend and at his Death he Left them Sumthing to live on and by his Will Recomended them to ye care of us undernamed they having no parents." From Wexford, Ireland, dated 12 mo. 5, 1704. Received 4 mo. 29, 1705.

WILLIAM HARRISON, "who for some years past have dwelt in these parts and have bin convinced * * * amongst us." From Mo. Mtg. at the Clifts, in Maryland, dated 4 mo. 15, 1705. Received 5 mo. 27, 1705.

MARY WILSON, unmarried, daughter of John Wilson, of Greenridge, in Coldbeck, Cumberland, England, "who for som years past hath Lived as a Servant in this Citty," intends "to Return into her native Contry again and from thence (if nothing Lett) to Transport herselfe into pensilvania." From Mtg. in Dublin,

Ireland, dated 10 mo. 19, 1704. Also, another certificate from Coldbeck Mo. Mtg. Cumberland, dated 11 mo. 7, 1704, states that Mary Wilson, "hath lived for some years last past in the Citty of Dublin and now Returned to her fathers house." Thomas and John Wilson signed certificate. Received 11 mo. 25, 1705.

THOMAS STORY, minister, from Mo. Mtg. in London, "within ye walls," dated 9 mo. 9, 1698. Also another certificate dated 1 mo. 23, 1701–2, from Two Weeks' Mtg. in London, stating that he is clear in relation to marriage. Received 11 mo. 26, 1699.

NAOMI BERRY, unmarried, from Mo. Mtg. at ye house of Sara Stevens on Choptank [Maryland], dated 1 mo. 28, 1706. Original on file. At Phila., 4 mo. 28, 1706. Married George Gray.

PAUL WOOLLFE, from Mo. Mtg. at Dublin, dated 12 mo. 24, 1706–7. Received 12 mo. 28, 1706–7.

JAMES ESTAUGH, unmarried, from Mo. Mtg. of Felsted Division, in Essex, England, dated 2 mo. 14, 1702. At Phila., 11 mo. 31, 1706–7. Original preserved.

MARGARET THORPE, from Mo. Mtg. [at Rahway, New Jersey], dated 11 mo. 17, 1706–7. She has been with us "Ever Since we had ye Dissipline of truth Set up among us here." and "hath been Instrumental for ye good of her children in keeping them to meettings." Received 11 mo. 31, 1706.

JOSEPH BROWN, late of Cohansey, with wife Lucia, dated 2 mo. 29, 1706, from Salem Mo. Mtg., New Jersey. Received 3 mo. 31, 1706. Not recorded.

JACOB MINSHALL, son of Thomas Minshall, to marry Sarah Owen, daughter of Griffith Owen; dated 10 mo. 30, 1706, from Chester Mo. Mtg., Pa. Received 11 mo. 31, 1706–7. Not recorded.

ELIZABETH PALMER, unmarried; dated 12 mo. 27, 1706, from Bridgetown, in Barbadoes. At Phila., 6 mo. 29, 1707. Not recorded.

JOHN TANNER, a letter concerning him from Lurgan Meeting, Ireland, dated 12 mo. 26, 1706. He is now in Phila. and has married Mary Rea. Letter brought before the Mo. Mtg. 5 mo. 25, 1707. Not recorded.

EBENEZER LARGE, dated 6 mo. 6, 1707, from Mo. Mtg. at the Falls, Bucks Co., Pa. Not recorded.

THOMAS BRIAN [Bryant], Jr., to marry Susanna Hearn; dated 7 mo. 1, 1707, from Burlington Mo. Mtg., New Jersey. At Phila., 6 mo. 29, 1707. Not recorded.

ISAAC MINSHALL, son of Thomas and Margaret, to marry Rebecca Owen, daughter of Griffith Owen. Dated 7 mo. 29, 1707, from Chester Mo. Mtg., Pa. At Phila., 7 mo. 26, 1707. Not recorded.

ROBERT CHAMBERLAINE, unmarried, from Mo. Mtg. at Horsleydown, England, dated 2 mo. 3, 1706. Received 1 mo. 28, 1707.

JEREMIAH WILLIAMS, unmarried, from Mo. Mtg. on Rhode Island, dated 12 mo. 26, 1706. Received 1 mo. 28, 1707.

EDWARD SKULL, unmarried ("now Supposed in or about Pensilvania"), from Mtg. in Cork, Ireland, dated 1 mo. 9, 1706. He served his apprenticeship with John Dennis, a Friend of Cork. Said Skull wrote to John Dennis for a certificate of removal. Original on file. Received 3 mo. 30, 1707.

GUIAN STEPHENS, unmarried, of Loughgaul, Co. of Armagh, Ireland. From Mtg. at Bellyhagan, Ireland, dated 7 mo. 5, 1700. Received 2 mo. 25, 1701.

GEORGE CALVERT, from Mo. Mtg. held in Carlisle, England, dated 11 mo. 19, 1704. Certificate addressed to Friends in London. Received 12 mo. 22, 1707-8.

WILLIAM MASSON, from Quarterly Mtg. at Stafford, England, dated 2 mo. 3, 1705. Received 12 mo. 27, 1707-8.

DAVID BRITNALL, Jr., unmarried, "having formerly Lived amongst us and now residing at philadelphia," desires a certificate to latter place. From Chester Mo. Mtg., Pa. dated 12 mo. 23, 1707–8. Original on file. Received 12 mo. 27, 1707–8.

MARY MATHEWS, unmarried, "having Removed herselfe for your Province," of Penna. From Mo. Mtg. at Dolobran, Wales, dated 11 mo. 27, 1707. Received 9 mo. 26, 1708.

JOAN HUMPHRYS, unmarried, "Late Resident with you and being Recomended by you to friends in these parts * * * and now being willing to return to you againe hath Desired of us a Certificate Shee living and having Lived for Sum time past our our Dear friend William Penn his house at Ealingwch is within ye Compass of our monthly meeting." She "has gained a very good Carracter from her master and mistres with whom Shee came from you and hath continued ever since." From Mo. Mtg. at Hamersmith, Co. of Middlesex, England, dated 12 mo. 5, 1707. Received 8 mo. 29, 1708.

MARY CAMM, wife of John Camm, "has had her Residence in this Citty from her Childehood, has also been a member of our womans meeting for Severall years." Her husband desires to go with her. From Mtg. at Cork, Ireland, dated 6 mo. 23, 1708. Received 10 mo. 31, 1708.

ELIZABETH JACOB, wife of Caleb Jacob,

"has Lived in this Citty for about 7 years and have been a member of our womens meeting for a year or more." From Mtg. at Cork, dated 6 mo. 23, 1708. Received 9 mo. 26, 1708.

JOHN PEELL, unmarried, son of Luke Peell, of Loughgall, Ireland, from Mtg. at Ballyhagan, Province of Ulster, Ireland, dated 8 mo. 17, 1708. Received 11 mo. 28, 1708.

JOSEPH GRIFFITH, [Griffin in Minutes] from Mo. Mtg. at Newark [or Kennett] Co. of New Castle, now Delaware, dated 4 mo. 7, 1707. Original on file. Received 11 mo. 28, 1708.

SARAH ARMITT, whose parents are deceased. "She behaved her Selfe modestly for though severall young men did offer themselves to her yet we find not but Shee is clear from all." From Mtg. at Leek, England, dated 11 mo. 21, 1702–3. Mary Armitt signed the certificate.

WILLIAM GREEN, a young servant, unmarried. From Mtg. at Ballycane, Co. of Wicklow, Ireland, dated 6 mo. 8, 1708. Also a certificate for him from Dublin, dated 6 mo. 15, 1708. Received 9 mo. 26, 1708.

SUSANNA PACKER, of City of Bristol, single woman, from Mtg. at Bristol, England, dated 7 mo. 13, 1708. Received 4 mo. 24, 1709.

LYDIA PAINTER, daughter of Ann Pusey, from Chester Mo. Mtg., Pa., dated 8 mo. 27, 1707. Received 2 mo. 29, 1708.

GEORGE PARKER, and family, from Mo. Mtg. at Burlington, New Jersey, dated 4 mo. 6, 1709. Received 6 mo. 26, 1709.

ESTHER PARKER, from Mo. Mtg. at Burlington, New Jersey, dated 6 mo. 1, 1709. Received 6 mo. 26, 1709.

SAMUEL COMBE, "Late of ye Citty Corke Cooper having transported himselfe and family to Pensilvania at Such time as severall friends of this place were Removing to that Country and not knowing he Should goe with them then, they Layd their Intentions of going before our meeting time nor Season afterwards did not offer for his getting a Certificate to Cary with him wherefore Since his arrivall there he having writ unto a friend here to procure one for him.

Said Samuel being a Bristol man, "Came over into this Country with his wife Some time after ye Wars ended to settle in Corke and follow ye Cooping trade and although he was observed to be a Laborious painfull man ye world favoured him not with Success we hope and desire it may be better in that country where we Suppose workmen of that Calling are not So plenty as in this nor materials to worke on Soe hard to be obtained as here." Clear in relation to marriage. Received 2 mo. 28, 1710.

FRANCES CHANDERS, daughter of Edward and Frances Godwinn, to marry Robert Bonell, dated 9 mo. 13, 1707. At Phila., 8 mo. 31, 1707. Not recorded.

JOHN SHARP, unmarried, dated 11 mo. 8, 1707, from Mo. Mtg. held at the house of Thomas Shakle. Received 11 mo. 30, 1707–8. Not recorded.

THOMAS GODFREY to marry Lucy Russell, dated 12 mo. 23, 1707–8, from Abington Mo. Mtg., Pa. Received 11 mo. 30, 1707–08. Not recorded.

JOHN CROXTON, unmarried, dated 1 mo. 29, 1708, from Chester Mo. Mtg., Pa. Received 5 mo. 30, 1708. Not recorded.

TRUSTRUM ALLEN, on a religious visit, dated 3 mo. 3, 1708, from Mo. Mtg. in Shrewsbury, East Jersey. Not recorded.

SAMUEL MARRIOTT, unmarried, dated 10 mo. 6, 1708, from Mo. Mtg. at Burlington, New Jersey. Received 11 mo. 28, 1708. Not recorded.

JOHN MAULE, unmarried, dated 6 mo. 12, 1708, from Mo. Mtg. at Lynn, New England. Received 11 mo. 28, 1708. Not recorded.

CALEB JACOB, by trade a knife cutler, dated 6 mo. 23, 1708, from meeting at Cork, Ireland. Received 9 mo. 26, 1708. Not recorded.

JOHN CAMM, "by occupation something of ye combing trade & some other branch of that manufactory." His wife, two children, and servants ; dated 6 mo. 23, 1708, from Mtg. at Cork, Ireland. Received 9 mo. 26, 1708. A letter concerning him from Cork, dated 5 mo. 4, 1709. Not recorded.

JONATHAN COPPOCK, to marry Jane Owen, daughter of Griffith Owen ; dated 10 mo. 27, 1708, from Chester Mo. Mtg., Pa. Received 11 mo. 28, 1708. Not recorded.

JOHN HART, unmarried, dated 11 mo. 12, 1708, from Mo. Mtg. at Cecil, Md. At Phila., 10 mo. 31, 1708. Not recorded.

RICHARD MOORE, unmarried, dated 3 mo. 13, 1709, from Mo. Mtg. at West River, Md. At Phila., 2 mo. 29, 1709. Not recorded.

JOSEPH BOND, son of James and Ann Bond, of Wrose, near Bradford, wife and child ; dated 6 mo. 8, 1709, from Brighouse Mo. Mtg., Co. of York, England. Received 11 mo. 26, 1710. Not recorded.

CHRISTOPHER TOPPEN, from Mo. Mtg. of Richmond, held at Leyburn, Yorkshire, England, dated 12 mo. 13, 1707–8. He "Came ye fore part of this year and gives an account yt he had a Certificate from ye monthly meeting of Philadelphia, wch thorow hardship he met with at Sea he happened to Lose and now these are to Certifie unto all whom it may Concerne that" he is clear in relation to marriage. Received 10 mo. 29, 1704.

JAMES LOGAN, single man, "now of Pensilvania Late of this Citty have Desired a Certificate from this meeting." From Mtg. at Bristol, England, dated 12 mo. 9, 1701. Original on file.

NATHAN SHENTON, of Cosby, Leicestershire, England, Grocer, and family, from Quarterly meeting, in Leicestershire, dated 4 mo. 2, 1709. Received 8 mo. 27, 1710. He died soon after his arrival, leaving five children, the oldest about sixteen years and the youngest about ten months old.

HANNAH SHENTON, unmarried, "Lately belonging to our meeting at Sutton, in ye county of Leicester," England, dated 2 mo. 21, 1710.

JOHN HARPER, unmarried, from Quarterly Meeting at Herring Creek, dated 6 mo. 2, 1710. Original on file. Received 8 mo. 27, 1710.

CHRISTIAN ROBISON, "did belong to this

meeting Severall years." Husband's name not mentioned. From Abington Mo. Mtg., Pa., dated 6 mo. 26, 1709.

JOHN LARGE, to marry Sarah Corker; dated 7 mo. 7, 1709, from Mo. Mtg. at the Falls, Bucks Co. Pa. Received 7 mo. 30, 1709. Not Recorded.

EDWARD CADWALADER, to marry Rebecca Moore; dated 8 mo. 13, 1709, from Haverford Mo. Mtg., Pa. Received 8 mo. 28, 1709. Not Recorded.

SAMUEL LEVIS, to marry Hannah Stretch; dated 8 mo. 31, 1709, from Mo. Mtg. at Middletown, Bucks Co., Pa. At Phila. 8 mo. 28, 1709. Not Recorded.

WILLOUGHBY WARDER, Jr., to marry Sarah Boyer; dated 9 mo. 2, 1709, from Falls Mo. Mtg., Bucks Co., Pa. At Phila. 12 mo. 24, 1709–10. Not Recorded.

GILBERT FALCONER, unmarried, dated 9 mo. 9, 1709, from Mo. Mtg. at Cecil, Md. Received 10 mo. 30, 1709. Not Recorded.

ROBERT BAKER, son of Joseph, to marry Susanna Packer, daughter of Robert; dated 10 mo. 26, 1709. Received 10 mo. 30, 1709. Not Recorded.

JAMES CRAWFORD, unmarried, dated 10 mo. 19, 1709, from Duck Creek Mo. Mtg. Received 11 mo. 27, 1709. Not Recorded.

WILLIAM LINGARD, and wife, Mary, from Mo. Mtg. at Horsleydowne, in Southwark, England, dated 12 mo. 1, 1709–10. Received 5 mo. 28, 1710.

JAMES LANGLEY, unmarried, of Rumsey, in County of Southton, Taylor, son of William Langley, late of same place, deceased, from Mo. Mtg. at Southamton, England, dated 4 mo. 14, 1710. Received 8 mo. 27, 1710.

THOMAS FERRIS, unmarried, "to goe into pensilvania as a Servant with our Dear friend, Tho: Chalkley. From Mo. Mtg. at Milverton, County of Somersett, England, dated 12 mo. 20, 1709–10. Francis and Richard Ferris signed certificate. Received 7 mo. 29, 1710.

FRANCIS FERRIS, Jr., unmarried, to go to Penna. as a servant to Thomas Chalkley. From Mo. Mtg. at Milverton, Co. of Somersett, England, dated 12 mo. 20, 1709–10. Signed by Francis and Richard Ferris. Received 7 mo. 29, 1710.

WILLIAM DUNN, unmarried, son of Thomas Dunn, of Bristol City, England, Lastmaker, from Bristol Mtg., England, dated 1 mo. 26, 1711. Received 6 mo. 31, 1711.

OWEN ROBERTS, and wife, Ann, from Harford (Haverford) Mo. Mtg. held at Merion, 12 mo. 9, 1709–10. Original on file.

JAMES STEEL, unmarried, from Mo. Mtg. at Duck Creek, New Castle Co., upon Delaware, dated 4 mo. 18, 1711. Original on file.

PHILLIP FAUSCET, unmarried, from Mo. Mtg. at Briggflats near Sedbergh, Yorkshire, England, dated 12 mo. 27, 1710. Received 7 mo. 28, 1711,

SAMUEL HILLARY, unmarried, son of Henry Hilliary, of Wexford, in Co. of Wexford, Ireland, brought up a Friend. "When he was grown up his Desire was to go to Sea to wch his parents Consented, and put him apprentice to a friend, and he served him honestly to ye best of our knowledge and since he hath been out of his time he hath Continued at Sea, but some time agoe his uncle Thomas Cuppage a friend of good account with us Dyed, and left him part of his Reall Estate to ye value of a hundred pounds per annum, and he ye sayd Samuel hath further aquainted that he hath Intentions of mariage with one Jane Waterman in ye province of pensilvania to wch his parents have given there consent." From Mtg. in Wexford, dated 4 mo. 10, 1711. Received 9 mo. 30, 1711.

SAMUEL TAYLOR, from Abington Mo. Mtg., Pa., dated 3 mo. 28, 1711. About to marry Elizabeth Robinson. Original on file. At Phila. Mo. Mtg. 3 mo. 25, 1711.

JACOB SIMCOCK, from Chester Mo. Mtg.,

Pa., dated 4 mo. 25, 1711. About to marry Sarah Waln, dau. of Nicholas. Original on file. Received 9 mo. 29, 1711.

CHARLES BROCKDEN, from Middletown Mo. Mtg., Bucks Co., Pa., dated 12 mo. 7, 1711. Original on file. Received 12 mo. 29, 1711.

FRANCIS JONES and family, dated 6 mo. 19, 1711, from meeting at Redstone, Wales, "About 3 years agoe they came over here to Pembrodshire, from Ireland and ever since did belong to our monthly meeting at Redstone." Received 12 mo. 29, 1711.

SAMUEL JONES and wife, from Meeting at Haverford West, dated 7 mo. 21, 1711. "About 3 years past he came over here from Ireland 2 years of wch time he lived with his father * * * and with ye aprobation of friends maried." Received 12 mo. 29, 1711.

PETER WISHARD, to marry a daughter of Thomas Betson; dated 12 mo. 27, 1709–10, from Abington Mo. Mtg., Pa. At Phila. 12 mo. 24, 1709–10. Not Recorded.

THOMAS BRODGATE, to marry Christiann Armstrong, relict of William Armstrong, late of Wapping, Co. of Middlesex, Mariner, deceased. His father, John Broadgate, of Enfield, in the county aforesaid, tailor, gives his consent to the marriage in a certificate dated 4 mo. 27, 1710. Certificate, dated 5 mo. 26,

1710, from Mo. Mtg. at Tattenham. Received 10 mo. 29, 1710. Not Recorded.

SARAH MASSEY, wife of Samuel Massey, and daughter of Thomas Wight, of Cork; dated 7 mo. 18, 1710, from Mtg. in Cork, Ireland. Received 3 mo. 25, 1711. Not Recorded.

JANE MARRIOT, wife of Isaac Marriot, daughter of Richard and Jane Marsh, dated 2 mo. 2, 1712, from Mo. Mtg. at Gulershedge, Middlesex, England. At Philadelphia Mo. Mtg., 6 mo. 31, 1716, Jane Mariot, wife of Isaac of this city, requested a certificate in order ''to return back to her Native Country to see her Ancient Mother.'' Signed 7 mo. 28, 1716. Not Recorded.

JOSEPH TAYLOR, young and unmarried, son of John Taylor, of Birtchall, near Cork, dated 3 mo. 3, 1711, from Mo. Mtg. at Leek, Staffordshire, England. Received 12 mo. 29, 1711.

ENION WILLIAMS, unmarried, from Mo. Mtg. ''held at Sarah Steevens on Divideing Creek,'' [Choptank] dated 1 mo. 27, 1712. Received 11 mo. 25, 1711.

JOHN KNIGHT, unmarried, son of Thomas Knight, of Bandon co. of Cork, Ireland, dated 8 mo. 22, 1711, from meeting in Cork. He now resides in Philadelphia and has written to his father, Thomas Knight, in regard to his certificate. Received 1 mo. 28, 1712. Original on file.

THOMAS BOND, unmarried, "formerly of Lancashire [England] Husbandman and for severall years last past of this Citty now gone for America." Dated 11 mo. 14, 1711, from meeting in London, England. Original on file. Received 3 mo. 30, 1712.

JAMES LOWNS, wife, and children, have removed to Philadelphia. Dated 1 mo. 31, 1712, from Mo. Mtg. at Middletown. Received 3 mo. 30, 1712.

MARK CARLETON and family, dated 4 mo. 3, 1711, from Mo. Mtg. at Mountmellick, Ireland. He is "ye Son of an early Labourer (after ye breaking forth of ye Gospel day) in ye word and Testimony of our Lord Jesus, and his wife ye Daughter of honest friends of this meeting." Original on file. Received 8 mo. 25, 1711.

THOMAS BARNES, from Brigflats, Yorkshire, England. Received 7 mo. 28, 1711.

AARON GOFORTH, wife, son, Aaron, and two daughters, Sarah and Elizabeth, dated 7 mo. 12, 1711, from Mo. Mtg. at Horsley Down, Southwark, England. Children unmarried. Received 4 mo. 27, 1712.

ELEANOR DAVIS, unmarried, dated 12 mo. 4, 1711, from Mo. Mtg. at Sadbury, Gloucestershire, England. She has a sister, "Elizabeth Howell, wife of Reece Howell, of New Town in Cheshire," Pennsylvania, who has "given her much Encouragement to come unto her."

JAMES MORRIS, unmarried, dated 1 mo. 7, 1711–12, from Meeting, in Dublin, Ireland. Original on file. Received 5 mo. 25, 1712.

PETER OSBORNE, of Wolverhampton, Staffordshire, England, with wife, Judith, and children, dated 7 mo. 11, 1711, from Mo. Mtg. at Rugely, Staffordshire. Also in the same certificate are mentioned, THOMAS NICHOLS, wife Mary, and children, from Staffordshire, England. Among signers to certificate are, Charles Osborne and John Till. Received 6 mo. 29, 1712. Original on file.

JOHN CARPENTER, unmarried, of Wolverhampton, Staffordshire, England. Dated 11 mo. 7, 1711, from Mo. Mtg. at Stafford. A good report received "from ye family where he has Lived (allmost from his Childhood)" Received 7 mo. 26, 1712.

HENRY THOMPSON, from Brig House, Mo. Mtg., Yorkshire, England. Received 7 mo. 28, 1711.

WILLIAM HARVEY, of City of Worcester, England, malster, dated 12 mo. 8, 1712, from Mo. Mtg. at Worcester. Received 7 mo. 26, 1712.

THOMAS SPEAKMAN, unmarried, "late of Reading," Berkshire, England, dated 4 mo. 24, 1712, from Mo. Mtg. at Reading. He was educated by his father in the Truth. He went from Reading "to London and Remained there about 13 months [with] a Certaine tradesman who hath given us a very good account of his honesty and Sobriety." Elizabeth Speakman signed certificate. Received 9 mo. 29, 1712.

JAMES WATSON, a young man, unmarried, belonging to Sunderland Mtg., where he resided about eight years. From Mo. Mtg. at New Castle, England; dated 1 mo. 10, 1711–12. Original on file. Received 10mo. 26, 1712.

JAMES HADWIN, dated 4 mo. 6, 1712, from Mo. Mtg. at Kendall, Westmoreland, England. He removed, "himself, about nine or ten months ago hither [to Kendall] and brought a certificate from Lancaster monthly meeting wch gave us acount that he was born of believing parents and Educated from his Childhood among friends." Received 11 mo. 30, 1712.

THOMAS CANNON, and wife, dated 4 mo. 13, 1712, from Lavington Mo. Mtg., Co. of Wilts, England. Received 9 mo. 29, 1712.

JOSHUA BAKER " (who for Som years past hath dwelt in this Citty)," dated 2 mo. 13,

1712, from Mtg. in Waterford, Ireland. Original on file. Received 1 mo. 27, 1713.

JAMES HURD, unmarried, coming on business; dated 2 mo. 24, 1712, from Mo. Mtg. at Limington, Somersettshire, England. Received 9 mo. 29, 1712. Not recorded.

RICHARD WHITTEN, dated 11 mo. 26, 1712, from Abington Mo. Mtg., Pa.; to marry Elizabeth Jyliff. Received 11 mo. 30, 1712. Not recorded.

JOSEPH LOW, dated 3 mo. 11, 1713, from Mo. Mtg. at Newton, Gloucester Co., New Jersey; to marry Elizabeth Taylor, of Philadelphia. Not recorded. At Phila., 2 mo. 25, 1713.

JOHN SHIERS, now in Pennsylvania "having Children;" dated 2 mo. 21, 1715, from Mo. Mtg. at Marsden, Lancashire, England. Original on file. Received 6 mo. 30, 1717, when he is about to return to England. Not recorded.

MARY PACE, "an inhabitant of this City [Worcester] for ye most part of her time, but lately removed to Liverpool in Lancashire, being inclined to goe to Pennsilvania;" dated 1 mo. 6, 1715–16, from Mo. Mtg. at Worcester, England. Signed by John and Elizabeth Pace. The certificate is endorsed on the back "To Mary Pace att Richard Kenerdy

at Leverpool By Chester Bagg." Original on
file. Not recorded.

WILLIAM MOORE, unmarried, dated 2 mo.
13, 1712, from Mtg. in Waterford, Ireland.
James Moore signed certificate. Original on
file. Received 1 mo. 27, 1713.

RICHARD PARKS, shoemaker "(who for
Divers years Last past hath Sojourned amongst
us)" and two children, dated 4 mo. 17, 1711,
from Preparative Meeting at Liverpool, Lancashire, England. He is a son of Richard
Parks, a Friend of Swarthmore Meeting, "in
this County," and has been a widower several
years. Original on file. Received 2 mo. 25,
1713.

NICHOLAS PYLE, a certificate from Chichester (Concord) Mo. Mtg., Pa., dated 12
mo. 13, 1713, in order to marry Ann Webb,
of Philadelphia Mo. Mtg. Original on file.
At Phila., 1 mo. 27, 1713.

ROBERT LODGE, (wife and young child,)
"hath Lived within the Compass of this
monthly meeting but a Short time, Coming to
from Hartshaw Monthly Meeting in our County
we Also Received from the Sayd monthly
meeting a Certificate Touching his Clearness
of women in those parts as touching marriage
* * * and after Sum time he was married to
Ann his now wife who had been a Servant at
Swathmore within the Compass of our monthly

meeting." Dated 12 mo. 3, 1713, from Swathmore Mo. Mtg. in Furness, Lancashire, England. Received 3 mo. 29, 1713.

ELIZABETH WARTENBY " (lately Duckworth)" wife of Edward Whartenby, intends shortly to travel with her husband to Pennsylvania. Dated 11 mo. 7, 1712, from Mo. Mtg. at Devonshire House, London, England. Received 3 mo. 29, 1713.

SARAH LEE, a minister, daughter of William and Mary Lee, deceased, of London, dated 8 mo. 20, 1712, from Two Weeks Meeting, in London. Received 3 mo. 29, 1713.

ANN SMITH, daughter of John Smith, brazier, of Wellingborrow, Northamptonshire, England. Dated 8 mo. 1, 1712, from Mo. Mtg. at Wellingborrow.

RICHARD LEWIS, minister, wife ("stricken in years") and sons, Thomas and James. Dated 2 mo. 28, 1713, from Quarterly Meeting at Dolobran, Montgomeryshire, Wales. Received 5 mo. 31, 1713.

JOHN CHAMBERS and family, sons, John and William, unmarried. Dated 1 mo. 6, 1712–13, from Mo. Mtg. at York, England. Received 5 mo. 31, 1713.

RACHEL MERRICK, unmarried, dated 1 mo. 31, 1713, from Mo. Mtg. held at Frandly, Cheshire, England. Original on file.

ABIGAIL HETHERINGTON, unmarried, dated 1 mo. 17, 1711–12, from Mtg. in Dublin, Ireland.

JOHN and DAVID DAVIES, unmarried, sons of Richard and Ann Davies, of "Rhieddallt, in ye parish of Ruabon and County of Denby in Wales, (who are a family of good Repute amongst friends and others)." Dated 1 mo. 20, 1712–13, from Mo. Mtg. at Namptwich, Cheshire, England. Received 5 mo. 31, 1713.

JOHN OWEN, unmarried, son of Griffith Owen, who returns to Pennsylvania. Dated 1 mo. 17, 1712–13, from Mo. Mtg. at Hartshaw, Lancashire, England. Received 5 mo. 31, 1713.

RICHARD TOWNSEND and wife Ann, about to remove to Philadelphia. Dated 5 mo. 26, 1713, from Abington Mo. Mtg., Pa. Received 5 mo. 31, 1713.

RICHARD SUNBY, of Billater Lane, London, tailor, son of Richard Sunby of Hornton Rudly, Yorkshire, tailor, deceased, intending to remove to New England. Dated 5 mo. 13, 1713, from Two Weeks Mtg. in London, England. Received 11 mo. 29, 1713.

MORDECAI MOORE, who expects to remain in Philadelphia during the winter. Dated 8 mo. 23, 1713, from Mo. Mtg. at West River, Md. Received 10 mo. 25, 1713.

ROBERT HIND and wife Mary, dated 11 mo. 28, 1712, from Mo. Mtg. at Horsly Down, in Southwark, England. Received 4 mo. 26, 1713.

JOSEPH COOPER, son of Joseph Cooper, of Cooper's Point, certificate in order for marriage with Mary Hudson, daughter of William Hudson, of Philadelphia. Dated 6 mo. 10, 1713, from Mo. Mtg. held at Thomas Shakles', in Gloucester Co., New Jersey. Original on file. At Phila., 5 mo. 31, 1713.

MARTHA ZEALY, "having a brother in your parts who by Invitation hath Induced her to Come to him." Dated 1 mo. 9, 1712, from Mo. Mtg. at Nailsworth, Co. of Gloucester, England.

JOHN WRIGHT, wife Patience, and four children. Dated 1 mo. 16, 1713–14, from Hartshaw Mo. Mtg., Lancashire, England. Received 5 mo. 30, 1714.

WILLIAM CLARE of Northwich, co. of Chester, England, wife, a minister, and family, members of Frandley Meeting. Dated 1 mo. 2, 1713–14, from Mo. Mtg. at Newton, Cheshire. Original on file. Received 5 mo. 30, 1714.

ELIZABETH HOLLIDAY, unmarried, of Nailsworth, co. of Gloucester, England. Dated 2 mo. 8, 1714, from Mo. Mtg. at Painsiorck(?), co. of Gloucester.

MARY DANE, unmarried, of Nailsworth, co. of Gloucester, England, dated 12 mo. 10, 1713–14, from Mo. Mtg. at Tedbury, co. of Gloucester.

WILLIAM CLIFTON and wife, dated 10 mo. 31, 1712, from Mo. Mtg. at Horslydown, in Southwark, England. He came into "the compass of our meeting and married his wife among us being ye daughter of an honest friend." Received 4 mo. 26, 1713.

JOSEPH BUCKLEY, unmarried, son of Joseph Buckley, late of London, linen draper, deceased. Dated 1 mo. 23, 1712, from Two Weeks Mtg. in London, England. Received 1 mo. 26, 1714.

JOHN LANCASTER, unmarried, "Came about ten years agoe out Cumberland into this nation (his parents being deceased) and was convinced of Truth amongst us about three years after." Dated 4 mo. 3, 1711, from Mo. Mtg. of Mountmellick, Ireland. Received 1 mo. 26, 1714.

HUGH CLIFTON, unmarried, of Wellingborrow, Co. of Northamptonshire, England, son of Hugh Clifton, of Sherington, in Buckinghamshire. Has father and mother's consent to remove. Certificate signed by Hugh and Mary Clifton. Dated 11 mo. 1, 1712, from Mo. Mtg. at Arthingborrow, Northamptonshire. Received 6 mo. 28, 1713.

MERCY PEARCE, daughter of Richard Pearce, of Parish of Aldersgate, London, deceased. Dated 6 mo. 10, 1713, from Two Weeks Meeting in London, England. Received 11 mo. 29, 1713.

SAMSON CORY, of Wootten Vuderedg, co. of Gloucester, England, and wife. Dated 1 mo. 11, 1713–14, from Mo. Mtg. at Naylsworth, co. of Gloucester. Received 5 mo. 30, 1714.

ABIGAIL ANTILL, unmarried, of Nailsworth, Co. of Gloucester, England. Dated 1 mo. 11, 1713–14, from Mo. Mtg. at Nailsworth. James Antill signed certificate.

JOHN NAILER "having proposed for a Certificate in order to proceed in marriage among you with Mary Greenhope we have made Enquiry acording to order and do find that Since he is Settled near Gweynedd wch is about two years that he often frequented there meeting and has ye Caracter of a good neighbor among them." Dated 10 mo. 7, 1713, from Radnor Mo. Mtg., Pa. Original on file. Received 7 mo. 25, 1713.

BENJAMIN BRIAN, certificate in order for marriage, from Burlington Mo. Mtg., N. J., dated 6 mo. 2, 1714. Original on file. At Phila., 5 mo. 31, 1714.

JAMES LOGAN, "an Inhabitant of your

Citty [Philadelphia] who Lately Resided here
has by a Letter to Henry Gouldney Requested
a certificate of his conversation and clearness
with Respect to marriage." Dated 5 mo. 13,
1713, from Two Weeks Meeting at Devonshire
House, London, England. Original on file.
Received 8 mo. 29, 1714.

ISAAC BARTON, of Clonmell, cutler, and
family, dated 3 mo. 16, 1714, from Six Weeks
Mtg. at Killcomonbegg, Ireland. Received
8 mo. 29, 1714.

DOROTHY BUMSTIDE. "John Hopes having
Received a letter from Elizabeth Whornaby
dated Philadelphia the 17th of the 5th month
1713 whereby She Requested a Certificate for
kinswoman Dorothy Bumstede Relating to her
Conversation and clearness as to marriage She
being Removed with Elizabeth Whornaby into
Pennsilvania." Dated 10 mo. 28, 1713, from
Two Weeks Meeting, London, England. Original on file.

FRANCIS EROTT, unmarried, a Friend by
birth. His father consents to his removal.
His mother is deceased. William Erott signed
certificate. Received 11 mo. 28, 1714.

JOANNA MEADE, unmarried, "Late of Col-
lumstock in ye County of Down," England.
Dated 11 mo. 26, 1712, from Mo. Mtg. at
Spirland (?). Also a certificate, dated 12 mo.

23, 1712–13, from Mtg. at Bristol, England, where she dwelt formerly.

ANN CHALKLEY, relict of Robert Chalkley, of Spittle Fields, in the Parish of Stepney, alias Stabonheath, Co. of Middlesex, weaver. Dated 2 mo. 18, 1715, from Two Weeks Mtg. in London. Original on file.

MARY FOWLER, unmarried, "having for Som years past lived within the Compass of this Meeting." Dated 12 mo. 8, 1714–15, from Mo. Mtg. at Horslydown, in Southwark, England.

KATHARINE MARTIN, "daughter in Law," of Sarah Martin (who acquainted the Peel Mo. Mtg. of the intention of her daughter-in-law to remove to Pennsylvania). Dated 1 mo. 7, 1714, from Two Weeks Meeting at Bull and Mouth, London, England. Original on file.

JACOB SHOEMAKER, wife Margaret, and children: Thomas, Jacob, and Susanna. Dated 12 mo. 28, 1714–15. Received 1 mo. 25, 1715.

WILLIAM CUMILL, of Morley, in the West Riding, of Co. of York, England. Dated 4 mo. 14, 1714, from Briggs House Mo. Mtg., held at Leeds, England.

JONATHAN COGSHALL, certificate for settlement and marriage with Martha Kite. Dated

8 mo. 13, 1715, from Haverford Mo. Mtg., Pa. Original on file. At Phila., 7 mo. 30, 1715.

JOSEPH KNIGHT, certificate in order for marriage with Abigail Antill, dated 8 mo. 31, 1715, from Abington Mo. Mtg. Pa. Original on file. At Phila. 8 mo. 28, 1715.

ALICE GOFORTH, "Daughter of Aaron Gofforth (Lately Removed unto your parts) She being about to Transport her selfe into America." Dated 1 mo. 23rd, 1714–15, from Mo. Mtg. at Horsleydown, in Southwark, England.

MARY GOFORTH, unmarried, dated 2 mo. 20, 1715, from Mo. Mtg. at Horslydown, in Southwark, England.

GEORGE SHIERS, a young man, unmarried, dated 1 mo. 5, 1714, from Brigghouse, Mo. Mtg., Yorkshire, England. Received 12 mo. 24, 1715.

HUGH PARSONS, "and Jane his wife Late of the Citty of Bath Removed hence in order to Settle at London but not getting any Buisness there to there Satisfaction we understand by Letter Sent down that they to go to Pensilvania." Dated 1 mo. 7, 1714–15, from Mo. Mtg. at Bath, Somersetshire, England. A certificate for *Henry* Parsons was produced at Phila. Mo. Mtg. 4 mo. 29, 1716.

JOSEPH BUCKLEY, unmarried, returning to

JOSEPH BUCKLEY, unmarried, returning to Philadelphia, dated 2 mo. 16, 1716, from Two Weeks Mtg. at Devonshire House, London, England. Received 4 mo. 29, 1716.

WILLIAM BISSELL, unmarried, of Duley, Co. of Worcester, England, and his four children. John Bissell signed certificate. From Storbridge Mo. Mtg. Original on file. Received 6 mo. 26, 1715.

MARTHA GRIFFITTS, "whose Husband Late being settled at Kingstown in Jamaica and hath wrote for his wife to come over to him, and she being willing to goo by An opertunity of Shiping that put into this Harbour by contrary winds bound to Jamaca." Dated 6 mo. 6, 1709, from Womens Meeting, in Cork, Ireland. She was born "of believing parents in this Citty." Frances Griffitts signed certificate. Original on file.

JOHN HEAD, dated 4 mo. 21, 1717, from Mo. Mtg. at Mildenhall, Co. of Suffolk, England. Original on file. Received 8 mo. 25, 1717.

CHRISTOPHER PENROSE, son of Robert and Mary, unmarried, brought up as a Friend and bound an apprentice to a Friend in Dublin. Dated 3 mo. 21, 1717, from Two Weeks Meeting at Dublin, Ireland. Original on file. Received 8 mo. 25, 1717.

THOMAS BARGER, wife and family, from

Meeting held in Clonmell, Co. of Tipperary, Ireland, dated 1 mo. 24, 1716–17. Original on file. Received 8 mo. 25, 1717.

EDWARD JONES, the younger, unmarried, a Friend by birth and "amongst us Excepting while he went two or three Voyages to Sea." Edward and Robert Jones signed certificate. Dated 10 mo. 12, 1717, from Radnor Mo. Mtg., Pa. Original on file. At Phila. Mo. Mtg., 10 mo. 27, 1717, Edward Jones, Jr. late of Merion Twp., produced a certificate.

RICHARD HOUGH, certificate in order for marriage with Deborah Gumly. Dated 7 mo. 4, 1717, from Mo. Mtg. at the Falls, Bucks Co., Pa. Original on file. Received 7 mo. 27, 1717.

JOSEPH GRAY, "son of our antient friend George Gray," certificate in order to marry Mary Hastings. Dated 7 mo. 30, 1717, from Abington Mo. Mtg., Pa. Original on file. At Phila., 7 mo. 27, 1717.

EDWARD OWEN, unmarried, son of Griffith Owen. Dated 6 mo. 20, 1717, from Hartshaw Mo. Mtg., in Lancashire, England, where he has been but a short time. Original on file. Received 11 mo. 31, 1717.

WILLIAM GROMETT, dated 4 mo. 20, 1717, from Mo. Mtg. at Wrangle, Lancashire, England. Received 2 mo. 25, 1718.

BENJAMIN DICKINSON, son of Roger and Deborah Dickinson, of Whitby, Co. of York, England. Dated 5 mo. 9, 1717, from Mo. Mtg. at Staintondale, for Scarborough, England. Received 3 mo. 30, 1718.

SARAH LEE, daughter of Thomas and Marth Lee, of London, England, deceased. Dated 1 mo. 17, 1717. Original on file.

JAMES WHITTON, a certificate in order to marry Katharine Bedwort; dated 3 mo. 26, 1718, from Salem Mo. Mtg., Salem Co., New Jersey. Original on file. At Phila., 3 mo. 30, 1718.

GEORGE SHOEMAKER and wife Rebecca, dated 6 mo. 29, 1715, from Abington Mo. Mtg., Pa. Received 4 mo. 29, 1716.

ANN NICHOLSON, of the Parish of Martins in the Fields, relict of Michael Nicholson, of the same place, carpenter, deceased. Dated 1 mo. 7, 1715–16, from Mo. Mtg. at the Savoy, London, England.

JOHN CARVER, of Byberry, certificate in order to marry Isabelle Welden, of Philadelphia Mo. Mtg. Dated 9 mo. 26, 1716, from Abington Mo. Mtg. Original on file. Received 8 mo. 26, 1716.

SAMUEL LEWIS, unmarried, son of Israel Lewis. Dated 7 mo. 20, 1716, from Mo. Mtg. at Bridgetown, on Barbadoes Island, West

Indies. In a letter, dated Barbadoes, ''ye 5th Sept. 1716,'' Israel Lewis gives his consent to the marriage of his son Samuel Lewis to Elizabeth Morris ''ye Daughter of Anthony Morris'' of Philadelphia. Original on file. Received 8 mo. 26, 1716.

THOMAS GRIFFITTS, unmarried, son of George Griffitts, of City of Cork, Ireland. Dated 8 mo. 16, 1716, from Mtg. at Cork. Also a certificate for Thomas Griffitts, from meeting in Kingston, Jamaica, dated 11 mo. 21, 1716. Among signers to latter certificate were: John Griffitts, Martha Griffitts and George Griffitts.

In a letter dated, Cork '' ye 17th of 8 mo., 1716,'' addressed to Isaac Norris and Jonathan Dickinson [in Philadelphia], George and Frances Griffitts write that their son, Thomas Griffitts, had written to them ''from ye bay of donna Maria'' that he was bound for Philadelphia. Original on file. Received 1 mo. 29, 1717.

WILLIAM TIDMARSH, dated 12 mo. 25, 1716, from Chester Mo. Mtg. Pa. Original on file. Received 8 mo. 26, 1716.

RICHARD HARRISON, Jr., unmarried, dated 9 mo. 16, 1716, from West River Mo. Mtg., Md. Original on file. Received 3 mo. 31, 1717.

ELIZABETH CULPIN, unmarried, ''having

Signified to us (by her master Wm. Collard Cheesmonger in wood Street) her Intention of Removing herselfe to Pennsylvania." Dated 7 mo. 24, 1711, from Two Weeks' Mtg. in London. Also a certificate, dated 9 mo. 16, 1716, from Mo. Mtg. at West River, Md., where she arrived from England and resided "for Som years" and now "being Some time past gone to your parts."

SOPHIA SIVERTS, late removed from Germantown to Philadelphia. Dated 2 mo. 29, 1717, from Abington Mo. Mtg., Pa. Original on file.

WALTER LONG, unmarried, of Whitechurch, co. of Dorset, where he has for some time resided, now about to return to America. Dated 5 mo. 25, 1695, from Mo. Mtg. at Topham, England.

DEBORAH GUMLEY, widow of John Gumley, and children, dated 6 mo. 26, 1716, from Duck Creek Mo. Mtg. She "Lived formerly amongst us together with her Said Husband, but hee her Said Husband not being in Unity with us, Took her ye said Deborah with him without Giving her an oppertunity to Apply her Selfe to us for a Certificate, but having so applyed herselfe Since her said Husbands Decease * * She Having Taken her former Husband amongst ffriends." At Phila., 7 mo. 27, 1717. Married Richard Hough at Phila., in 1717. Not recorded.

WILLIAM HINTON, now in Philadelphia, unmarried, dated 11 mo. 6, 1717, from Nailsworth, England. On the back of the certificate is a letter to William Hinton, from his father, John Hinton, in which he states: "your Sister Mary Harris Departed this Life in April Last & Soe did not See your Letter * * * Thomas ffreem Desires you to Remember his Love to Sampson Keary." "Joseph Prides ffather Brother and Sisters are well in Health and Desires to have their Dear Love Remembered to him." The certificate is endorsed: "ffor William Hinton to be Left for him att Joseph Prides Barber In Philadelphia America." Original on file. Not recorded. At Phila., 4 mo. 27, 1718.

JOSEPH WOOD and family, of Mountroth Particular Meeting, Ireland, dated 2 mo. 8, 1717, from Mountmellick Meeting, Ireland. He is a maker of parchment and glue. Original on file. Received 4 mo. 27, 1718.

RICHARD MARTIN, unmarried, of Kirkbride, dated 2 mo. 12, 1717, from Holme Mo. Mtg., Cumberland, England. Certificate signed by James and Lancelot Martin. Received 4 mo. 27, 1718.

HUMPHREY NORRIS, unmarried, late of Bristol, England, glazier; dated 12 mo. 17, 1717, from Bristol. Original on file. Received 4 mo. 27, 1718.

EBINEZER ROBINSON, JR., unmarried, brazier ; and late apprentice to Thomas Crawley ; dated 2 mo. 28, 1718, from Two Weeks' Meeting in London, England. Received 6 mo. 29, 1718.

SARAH LLOYD, widow of Thomas Lloyd, late of Goodman's Fields, merchant. Dated 12 mo. 17, 1717, from Two Weeks' Meeting, in London, England.

PETER LLOYD, unmarried (son of Thomas Lloyd), late of London, merchant. Dated 1 mo. 3, 1717–18, from Meeting in Bristol, England.

RICHARD SMITH, dated 9 mo. 11, 1718, from New Garden Mo. Mtg., Chester Co., Pa. He came to New Garden from Rhode Island.

WILLIAM TAYLOR, saddletree maker, now in Pennsylvania. Dated 1 mo. 24, 1716, from Meeting in Clonmell, County of Tipperary, Ireland. Original on file. Received 5 mo. 25, 1718.

THOMAS SKELTON, unmarried, dated 2 mo. 13, 1716, from Mo. Mtg. at Carlisle, in Cumberland, England. Original on file.

ANN PYLE, widow, dated 10 mo. 1, 1718, from Concord Mo. Mtg., Pa. Original on file.

ELIZABETH TOMLINSON, unmarried, "dwelt within ye Compass of Southurack Monthly Meeting about Six Years agoe." Dated 12 mo. 2, 1718, from Two Weeks' Meeting, London, England.

JAMES LLOYD and wife Ann, now in Pennsylvania, formerly belonging to Bewdley Meeting, County of Worcester, England. Dated 1 mo. 17, 1717-18, from Mo. Mtg. at Dudley, England. Original on file. Received 3 mo. 30, 1719.

HUGH CLIFTON, unmarried, returning to Philadelphia; dated 1 mo. 30, 1719, from Abington Mo. Mtg., Pa. Original on file. Received 2 mo. 24, 1719.

DANIEL FLEXNEY, unmarried, son of Daniel Flexney, of Burford, in County of Oxon; dated 6 mo. 11, 1718, from Witney Mo. Mtg.; John, John, Jr., and Daniel Flexney signed certificate. Original on file. Received 7 mo. 26, 1718.

JOHN WILSON, unmarried, about to return to Pa.; dated 12 mo. 17, 1718, from Hartshow, Mo. Mtg., Lancashire, England. Original on file.

THOMAS LINSLEY (Lindley in Minutes), unmarried, a smith, now in Philadelphia; dated 11 mo. 27, 1718, from Dublin, Ireland. Received 7 mo. 24, 1719.

EDWARD BROOKS, a certificate for settlement and marriage with Elizabeth Snead; dated 10 mo. 28, 1719, from Abington Mo. Mtg., Pa. Original on file. At Philadelphia, 9 mo. 27, 1719.

JANE IRELAND, wife of Nicholas Ireland, dated 10 mo. 2, 1719, from Darby Mo. Mtg., Pa. Original on file. Received 9 mo. 25, 1720.

ELIZABETH WHARTNABY, minister, on a religious visit; dated 5 mo. 27, 1719, from Mo. Mtg. on Nantucket. Original on file. Not recorded.

HESTER KINGSLEY, unmarried, returning to Pennsylvania; dated 6 mo. 25, 1719, from Mo. Mtg. at Portsmouth, Rhode Island. Not recorded.

MARY RAKESTRAW, dated 5 mo. 11, 1720, from Mo. Mtg. at Newton, New Jersey. Received 7 mo. 30, 1720. Not recorded.

SARAH FISHER, dated 7 mo., 1721, from Burlington, N. J. Received 9 mo. 24, 1721. Not recorded.

ELIZABETH TEOGUE, returning from a religious visit, in company with Margaret Pain. Dated 5 mo. 14, 1721, from Quarterly Mtg. held at Newport, Rhode Island. Not recorded.

THOMAS WHITEHEAD, unmarried, of Breadstreet, London, son of Henry Whitehead, late of same place, deceased. He has been in membership with Friends about three years. Dated 9 mo. 9, 1719, from Two Weeks' Meeting, in London, England. Original on file. Received 2 mo. 29, 1720.

HANNAH ALBINSON, widow, dated 2 mo. 25, 1720, from Abington Mo. Mtg., Pa. Received

WILLIAM ADAMS, unmarried, dated 1 mo. 30, 1720, from Mo. Mtg. in Bridge Town, Barbadoes Island. Original on file.

JOHN BROWNE and wife, late of Barking, County of Essex, England, "Transported themselves to Pensilvania," about "17 or 18 years" ago. Dated 5 mo. 4, 1718, from Mo. Mtg. at Barking. Original on file. Received 3 mo. 27, 1720.

MARY NOBLE, dated 3 mo. 2, 1720, from Burlington Mo. Mtg., New Jersey.

JOSEPH ELGAR, and wife, Margaret, of Folkstone, County of Kent, England ; dated 2 mo. 12, 1720. Certificate signed by John Elgar, Sr., Margaret Elgar, and Mary Elgar. Original on file. Received 7 mo. 30, 1720.

SAMUEL OVERTON, JR., unmarried, about to take a voyage for purposes of trade to America. Dated 8 mo. 7, 1719, from Mo. Mtg. in City of Coventry, County of Warwick,

England. Certificate signed by Samuel Overton, Sr., and Mary Overton. Original on file.

ELIZABETH LARGE, dated 6 mo. 7, 1720, from Falls Mo. Mtg., Bucks Co., Pa. Original on file. Received 6 mo. 26, 1720.

WILLIAM DUNN, unmarried, dated 8 mo. 3, 1720, from Burlington Mo. Mtg., New Jersey. Certificate addressed to Friends of City of Bristol, England, he intending to transport "himself to his native Land, his former place of abode." Original on file. Received 9 mo. 25, 1720.

THOMAS PENNINGTON, certificate in order to marry a daughter of James Steele. Dated 3 mo. 29, 1721, from Abington Mo. Mtg., Pa. Original on file. Received 4 mo. 30, 1721.

JOHN LAWSON, of Nailsworth, England, a professed minister of the Society, was at Philadelphia, 9 mo. 24, 1721, but not bringing a certificate of removal, he is not received a member of Phila. Mo. Mtg.

MARY ELLIS, dated 12 mo. 2, 1720, from Mo. Mtg. at Chesterfield, Burlington Co., N. J. Original on file.

JOHN REEVES, of Whitby, County of York, mariner. Dated 1 mo. 1, 1719-20, from Mo. Mtg. at Scarborough, held at Whitby, England. Original on file.

MARY TOMPKINS, relict of John Thompkins, deceased, and her son, John. Dated 6 mo. 15, 1720, from Two Weeks' Mtg. in London, England. Original on file.

THOMAS DENHAM, unmarried; dated 12 mo. 20, 1715-16, from Mtg. in Bristol, England, He "having Resided near the Citty about three quarters of a year." A certificate, dated 1 mo. 21, last, has already been sent and is in the hands of Jonathan Dickinson. Received 6 mo. 25, 1721.

AMY LIBERTY, unmarried, dated 9 mo. 20, 1719, from Mo. Mtg. at Market street, County of Hartford, "for ye Service of Truth in ye uper Side of ye County of Bedford," England. "Shee having Lived part of her time Since her Childhood from us." Also a letter, dated 7 mo. 18, 1719, from George Chalkley, Jr., of Edmonton, her kinsman. Married Joshua Lawrence, at Philadelphia, 1722.

JOHN STAMPER, a young man, dated 7 mo. 18, 1722, from Mo. Mtg. at Pardshaw Cragg, Cumberland, England. He "hath come amongst friends for Severall years past." Original on file. Received 4 mo. 28, 1723.

SAMUEL BOULTON, wife, and family, have removed themselves within the limits of Philadelphia Mo. Mtg. Dated 2 mo. 30, 1721, from Abington Mo. Mtg., Pa. Certificate signed by Everad, Margaret and Rebecca Boulton. Received 3 mo. 25, 1722.

THOMAS OLIVER, "our old friend," unmarried ; dated 12 mo. 25, 1723, from Mo. Mtg. at Dolobran, Wales. He "hath Removed himself into your parts Sometime agoe." Received 4 mo. 26, 1724.

JOSEPH (husbandman), JOSHUA, ANN, and RACHEL RICHARDSON, brothers and sisters, all unmarried. Dated 12 mo. 7, 1723-4, from Richmond Mo. Mtg. held at Chantrey, County of York, England. Received 4 mo. 26, 1724.

EDWARD HORNE, and wife Elizabeth (a minister) ; dated 10 mo. 10, 1723, from Quarterly Mtg. held at Horsham, County of Sussex, England. Original on file. Received 5 mo. 31, 1724.

RALPH HOY, unmarried, "an Irishman having lived three years and a half with a friend of our meeting." Dated 12 mo. 7, 1724, from Richmond Mo. Mtg., held at Chantrey, County of York, England. Received 12 mo. 25, 1725.

GEORGE and ELIZABETH DEEBLE, children of Richard Deeble, of Cork, deceased. The father died "about three years and a halfe [ago] and Left nine small children behinde him, over whom ye care of friends of this Citty for theire good has not been wanting and Some of theire near Relations in Pensilvania having Lately given Some Encouragement to Receive Some of them if they were Sent thither, the above named George and Elizabeth ye two Eldest were very Desirous to go with a younger Sister." Dated 2 mo. 23, 1722, from Mtg. at Cork, Ireland. Received 6 mo. 31, 1722. Original on file.

MARY MILLER, and son, James Miller; dated 11 mo. 23, 1723-4, from Mo. Mtg. at Carlisle, Cumberland, England. "Ye sayd James Miller being ye only Son and heire to James Miller, Deceased, ye husband of ye Sayd Mary Miller and has a Legall Right to an Estate or Share of a propriety in your parts being the purchase of his Sayd father, James Miller, Deceased." Original on file. Received 9 mo. 27, 1724.

WILLIAM SANDERS, unmarried, dated 1 mo. 26, 1722, from Two Weeks' Mtg. in London, England. He produced a certificate to London from Philadelphia, dated 5 mo. 29, 1720, and is now returning to Philadelphia. Original on file.

GRIFFITH OWEN, dated 12 mo. 22, 1724, from Two Weeks' Mtg. in London, England. He produced a certificate, dated 1 mo. 30, 1723, from Philadelphia to London, and is now returning to Philadelphia. Original on file.

ESTHER TOMLINSON, unmarried; dated 11 mo. 3, 1721, from Darby Mo. Mtg., Pa. Original on file. Not recorded.

JOSEPH ENGLAND, SR., to marry Elizabeth Brown ; dated 9 mo. 20, 1721, from Duck Creek Mo. Mtg., Delaware. Original on file. Not recorded. Received 11 mo. 26, 1721.

SARAH GRISCOM ; dated 12 mo. 12, 1721–2, from Mo. Mtg. at Newton, New Jersey. Received 8 mo. 25, 1723. Not recorded.

SAMUEL OGDEN and wife Hester ; dated 12 mo. 26, 1721–2, from Chester Mo. Mtg., Pa. Received 1 mo. 30, 1722. Not recorded.

MARY OLDMAN, dated 1 mo. 1, 1722, from Darby Mo. Mtg., Pa. Received 1 mo. 30, 1722. Not recorded.

HANNAH COFFIN, dated 1 mo. 12, 1721–2, from Mo. Mtg. held at Newton, New Jersey. Received 1 mo. 30, 1722. Not recorded.

ISAAC MARRIOT, and wife Jane; dated 1 mo. 7, 1722, from Mo. Mtg. of Hendon, in Middlesex, England. Original on file. Not recorded.

JOHN SMITH, unmarried, dated 1 mo. 26, 1722, from Mo. Mtg. at Salem, New Jersey. At Philadelphia, 12 mo. 23, 1721. Not recorded.

WILLIAM GARRETT, who has "lived amongst us Thirty and seven years and is now in his old age removed to Philadelphia." Dated 5 mo. 4, 1722, from Darby Mo. Mtg., Pa. Received 5 mo. 27, 1722. Not recorded.

MARY PRESTON, "Daughter of our Antient friends William and Jane Bedward, being Born, Educated, brought up and maried among us, and was amongst us the most of her life time, excepting Some years She has lived elsewhere with the consent of her mother." Dated 6 mo. 9, 1722, from Merion Mo. Mtg., Pa. Received 6 mo. 31, 1722. Not recorded.

FRANCES BURD, unmarried, dated 11 mo. 28, 1722–3, from Chester Mo. Mtg., Pa. Not recorded.

MARTHA MACDONNELL, dated 3 mo. 27, 1723, from Chester Mo. Mtg., Pa. "Several of us have known her from a Child, she being Bound out very young and as we understand During her Servitude she Discharged her Duty to ye Satisfaction of her Master and Mistress." Received 3 mo. 31, 1723. Not recorded.

MARY COOPER, widow, dated 4 mo. 5, 1723, from Mo. Mtg. at the Falls, Bucks Co., Pa. Received 6 mo. 30, 1723. Not recorded.

HANNAH ALBERSON, dated 4 mo. 10, 1723, from Haddonfield Mo. Mtg., New Jersey. She came to Haddonfield from Byberry Mo. Mtg., Pa. At Phila., 3 mo. 31, 1723. Not recorded.

ANN ROBERTS and SUSANNA MORRIS, on

a religious visit, dated 6 mo. 13, 1723, from Nansemond, Virginia. Not recorded.

ANN CLIFTON, unmarried, dated 2 mo. 13 and 14, 1724, from Mtg. in Dublin, Ireland. Returning to Philadelphia from a visit to Ireland.

JOHN BENSON and wife Mary, and family ; dated 2 mo. 6, 1725, from Mo. Mtg. at Frandley, Cheshire, England. They brought a certificate to Frandley from Lancashire. Received 9 mo. 26, 1725.

ANN FARMER, of Saffron Walden, daughter of John and Mary Farmer. Dated 12 mo. 23, 1724, from Mo. Mtg. at Saffron Walden, County of Essex, England. Signed by Mary Farmer. Original on file. Received 7 mo. 24, 1725.

LETTICE SWIFT, unmarried, who has lived as a servant for several years with John Fream ; dated 6 mo. 30, 1721, from Mo. Mtg. at Endfield, County of Middlesex, England. Received 3 mo. 27, 1726.

REBECCA GRAY, daughter of Thomas Gray, dated 2 mo. 1, 1725, from Mo. Mtg. at Ratclife, London, England. Received 3 mo. 27, 1726.

LLOYD ZACHARY, unmarried, dated 5 mo. 26, 1725, from Two Weeks Mtg. in London,

England. He is returning to Philadelphia, Received 2 mo. 29, 1726.

MARY GRAY, widow, dated 7 mo. 30, 1723, from Abington Mo. Mtg., Pa. Received 9 mo. 29, 1723. Not recorded.

SARAH WORTHINGTON, wife of Daniel, dated 11 mo. 9, 1723–4, from Haverford Mo. Mtg., Pa. Received 2 mo. 29, 1726. Not recorded.

DANIEL EVANS, and wife, Emin, the latter a minister, dated 2 mo. 27, 1724, from Abington Mo. Mtg., Pa. Received 3 mo. 29, 1724. Not recorded.

EDWARD BEAKES, unmarried, dated 4 mo. 4, 1724, from Chesterfield Mo. Mtg., Burlington Co., N. J. At Phila., 3 mo. 29, 1724. Not recorded.

ELIZABETH LARGE, widow, dated 4 mo. 4, 1724, from Chesterfield Mo. Mtg., New Jersey. At Phila., 3 mo. 29, 1724. Not recorded.

MARY ROBERTS, dated 7 mo. 10, 1724, from Radnor Mo. Mtg., Pa. Not recorded.

HANNAH BRINTNALL, dated 1 mo. 1, 1724, from Burlington Mo. Mtg., New Jersey. Received 6 mo. 27, 1725. Not recorded.

ANN TATNELL, widow, and her son, Thomas

Tatnell, dated 1 mo. 26, 1725, from Quarterly Mtg. at Leicester, England. Not recorded.

BRIDGET JACKSON, a young woman, dated 2 mo. 20, 1725, from Mo. Mtg. at Pardshaw Cragg, Cumberland, England. Not recorded.

SARAH HODGSON, dated 5 mo. 7, 1725, from Falls Mo. Mtg., Bucks Co., Pa. Received 5 mo. 30, 1725. Not recorded.

RALPH HOY, unmarried, dated 12 mo. 3, 1725–6, from Middletown Mo. Mtg., Bucks Co., Pa. Received 12 mo. 25, 1725. Not recorded.

JOHN IDEN and wife, Hannah (a minister), dated 2 mo. 25, 1726, from Chester Mo. Mtg., Pa. Not recorded.

MARY FINLOW, to return to Phila., dated 3 mo. 25, 1726, from Limerick, Ireland. Not recorded.

CATHARINE WISTER, dated 9 mo. 28, 1726, from Abington Mo. Mtg., Pa. Received 10 mo. 30, 1726. Not recorded.

ROBERT WOODCOCK, of Lambstown, co. of Welford, Ireland, and wife, who is a daughter of Jacob and Ruth Barcroft. Dated 1 mo. 12, 1727, from Cooledine Mtg., Ireland. Not recorded.

JACOB HORNOR, to marry, dated 4 mo. 12,

1727, from Haddonfield Mo. Mtg., N. J. Original on file. Received 5 mo. 28, 1727. Not recorded.

MARY CARLILE and daughter Sarah Carlile, late inhabitants in "our town of Burlington, butt now Rem [oved from] us to Inhabit within your City of Philadelphia." Dated 12 mo. 5, 1727–8, from Burlington, N. J. Original on file. Received 1 mo. 29, 1728. Not recorded.

JOHN PASCHALL, to marry Frances Hodge. Dated 1 mo. 6, 1727–8, from Darby Mo. Mtg., Pa. At Phila., 12 mo. 23, 1727–8. Not recorded.

ELIZABETH NICHOLSON, unmarried, dated 2 mo. 20, 1725, from Mo. Mtg. at Pardshaw Cragg, in Cumberland, England. Received 2 mo. 29, 1726.

REBECCA RITSON, unmarried, dated 2 mo. 20, 1725, from Mo. Mtg. at Pardshaw Cragg, in Cumberland, England. Jeremiah Cowman signed the certificate. Received 2 mo. 29, 1726.

MARY SMITH and daughter Mary, unmarried, dated 5 mo. 5, 1726, from Mo. Mtg. at Bridgetown, Barbadoes Island, West Indies. Received 6 mo. 26, 1726.

MARY RAPER, unmarried, dated 2 mo. 27, 1726, from Mo. Mtg. at Bridgetown, Barbadoes. Received 7 mo. 30, 1726.

JOSEPH WOOD, unmarried, son of Joseph Wood, deceased. Dated 4 mo. 7, 1727, from Falls Mo. Mtg., Bucks Co., Pa. He is returning to Philadelphia from service as an apprentice at Falls. Original on file. Received 4 mo. 27.

JOHN WALBY and wife SUSANNA, dated 2 mo. 10, 1728, from Mtg. at Moat, Ireland. "He was born in England, & came unto this Nation [Ireland] in the Nature of a Scool Master. And first Settled with our ffrd Samuel Wattson in the County of Caterbough, where he removed for Som years, till he maried Susannah Russell Daughter to our ffrd. John Russell, of this Meeting. And lived amongst us more than a year, during which time his behaveiour has been orderly, he allso brought us good Certificates both from England and Carlow Mens Meeting." Signed by Mary Russell and two John Russells. Received 7 mo. 27, 1728.

DEBORAH CORDRY, wife of Hugh Cordry; dated 10 mo. 27, 1700, from Mo. Mtg. at Ratclif, England.

WILLIAM CALLENDER, JR., unmarried, being about to take business voyage to Philadelphia. Dated 1 mo. 2, 1726–7, from Mo. Mtg. at Hethcots Bay, Barbadoes. Original on file. Received 2 mo. 28, 1727.

RICHARD ARMITT, son of John Armitt,

dated 8 mo. 2, 1701, from Mo. Mtg. at Leek, Staffordshire, England. The said Richard Armitt transported himself to America in 1700, and by letter asked for a certificate. He "has lived for some years from amongst us & hath followed his trade in London and has been some Voyages in Spain, &c." His father is living but his mother is dead. John Armitt, the father; John Armitt, a brother; Sarah Armitt and Mary Armitt signed the certificate. In a postscript to the certificate the father mentions "my brother Robt. Heath." At Phila., 5 mo. 25, 1701.

THOMAS JANNEY, unmarried, "late a member of this meeting having transported himself into yt province [Penna.] and by our frd. Randle Janney his Brother" desires a certificate. He "was born of and brought up by beleiving Parents." Dated 9 mo. 4, 1702, from Mo. Mtg. at Morley, in Pownelfee, Cheshire, England.

JOHN SHIERS, dated 2 mo. 21, 1715, from Mo. Mtg. at Marsden, England. Now in Pennsylvania. Received 6 mo. 30, 1717.

MARY DAVIS, widow of John Davis ; dated 6 mo. 22, 1722, from Quarterly Meeting at Eversham, Worcestershire, England. Original on file. Received 12 mo. 22, 1722.

ROBERT ROBERTSON, son of Samuel Robertson, merchant, in this place. Dated 6 mo. 20,

1727, from Mo. Mtg. at Kelso [an island]. Signed by Samuel, Thomas and David Robertson. Original on file.

JOSEPH FRENCH, dated 2 mo. 13, 1727, from Mo. Mtg. at Bridgetown, Barbadoes. He is about to take a voyage to Pennsylvania. He has a son Joseph. Original on file.

RICHARD BURTOS, dated 7 mo. 5, 1728, from Mo. Mtg. at Chesterfield, New Jersey. Now settled in Penn'a. Original on file. Received 5 mo. 25, 1729.

JACOB VERNON, wife Elinor, and children; dated 11 mo. 27, 1728–9, from Chester Mo. Mtg., Pa. Original on file. Received 12 mo. 28, 1728–9.

THOMAS PERRY [Parry], unmarried; dated 3 mo. 19, 1729, from Two Weeks' Mtg. at Colchester, co. Essex, England. Original on file. Received 1 mo. 30, 1733.

GEORGE HOWELL and wife, dated 2 mo. 28, 1729, from Mtg. at Cork, Ireland. Signed by Charles Howell. Original on file.

JOHN WELTON, wife and family; dated 10 mo. 28, 1724, from Bristol, England. Now removed to Penn'a. Original on file. Endorsed by Radnor Mo. Mtg., Pa., 10 mo. 12, 1728. Received 11 mo. 31, 1728.

SARAH MARSHALL, daughter of Richard

and Deborah Marshall, dated 4 mo. 1, 1729, from Mo. Mtg. at Edenderry, Ireland. Original on file. Received 6 mo. 29, 1729.

THOMAS BAYNES and wife Jennet; dated 3 mo. 1, 1729, from Mo. Mtg. at Middletown, Bucks Co., Pa. Original on file.

ABRAHAM ENGLAND, unmarried, son of Joseph England. Dated 2 mo. 22, 1728, from Duck Creek Mo. Mtg., Delaware. Received at Phila., 2 mo. 26, 1728. Not recorded.

SUSANNA BICKLY, daughter of Abraham Bickley, deceased ; dated 4 mo. 3, 1728. At Phila., 3 mo. 31, 1728. Not recorded.

MICHAEL POINCE, to marry Elizabeth Nicholson. Dated 4 mo. 24, 1728, from Abington Mo. Mtg., Pa. At Phila., 4 mo. 28, 1728. Not recorded.

ELIZABETH TOWNSEND, dated 4 mo. 24, 1728, from Abington Mo. Mtg., Pa. Not recorded.

WILLIAM MORRIS, on business, dated 7 mo. 5, 1728, from Mo. Mtg. at Heathcot's Bay, in Barbadoes. Received 12 mo. 28, 1728–9. Not recorded.

REBECCA BOLTON, dated 7 mo. 30, 1728, from Abington Mo. Mtg., Pa. Not recorded.

LOWRY SYDDON and family, dated 11 mo. 28, 1728–9, from Gwynedd Mo. Mtg., Pa. Not recorded.

JOB GOODSON, returning to Penna.; dated 2 mo. 2, 1729, from Mo. Mtg. at Horsleydown, in Southwark, England. Received 8 mo. 31, 1729. Not recorded.

THOMAS CHALKLEY, a traveling minister, dated 3 mo. 15, 1729, from Mo. Mtg. in Bridgetown, Barbadoes. Not recorded.

WILLIAM CALLENDER, JR., unmarried, on business; dated 3 mo. 21, 1729, from Mo. Mtg. at Heathcot's Bay, Barbadoes. Received 5 mo. 25, 1729. Not recorded.

HANNAH and ESTHER WOOLMAN, daughters of John Woolman, late of Burlington Co., N. J., deceased. Dated 5 mo. 7, 1729, from Burlington Mo. Mtg., N. J. Not recorded.

GEORGE FRANCKS and wife Elizabeth (who brought her certificate from England); dated 5 mo. 28, 1729, from Abington Mo. Mtg., Pa. Original on file. Received 6 mo. 29, 1729.

WILLIAM LITGREAVES and wife; dated 6 mo. 13, 1729, from Bull and Mouth Mo. Mtg., London, England. Original on file. Received 6 mo. 26, 1729.

LETTICE HATTON, unmarried; dated 5 mo. 29, 1729, from Mtg. in Dublin, Ireland. She was not brought up as a Friend, but "has lived about seven years a Servant to Sundry friends in this City who give a good report of her, she having been five years & half in the frd's service in wch she is now likely to remove and for about four years past has frequented our Religious Meetings * * * her own Father is dead, but her Mother being living Consents to her Going." Original on file. Received 2 mo. 24, 1730.

JOHN LOW, unmarried, "hath lived severall years servant to Robert Greer & his Son John till of late he removed himself to Lurgon." Dated 2 mo 11, 1722, from Mtg. at Grange, near Charlemount, co. of Armagh, Ireland. Also a certificate dated 3 mo. 7, 1729, from Mtg. at Lurgon, co. of Antrim, Ireland. Original on file.

ANN GOODBODY, dated 5 mo. 29, 1729, from Dublin Mtg., Ireland. Received 10 mo. 26, 1729. Not recorded.

ANN CUNNINGHAM, and niece Ann, unmarried; dated 5 mo. 29, 1729, from Dublin Mtg., Ireland. The niece Ann Cunningham is about sixteen years of age and "Goes over as Apprentice or Servant to and along with our Friend Thomas Millhouse and his wife. Also Elizabeth and Mary Cunningham, the small sisters of the niece Ann go with her." Original on file. Received 10 mo. 26, 1729. Not recorded.

MARY BOYES, daughter of Jacob and Lucy Turner, was married 6 mo. 17, 1720, in the Meeting House at Lurgon, Ireland, to John Boyes. Dated 5 mo. 30, 1729, from Lurgon Mtg., Ireland. Jane, Ann, Elizabeth, Sarah, John, Jacob, Thomas and Samuel Turner sign the certificate. Original on file. Received 11 mo. 30, 1729–30. Not recorded.

ANTHONY MORRIS, unmarried, nephew of William Morris. Returning to Penna. Dated 6 mo. 20, 1729, from Mo. Mtg. at Heathcott's Bay, Barbadoes, where he has been making a short stay. Not recorded.

WILLIAM WILLIAMS, to marry Hannah Carver. Dated 8 mo. 28, 1729, from Gwynedd Mo. Mtg., Pa. At Phila. 7 mo. 26, 1729. Not recorded.

ROSE BETHEL, widow of John Bethel, late of Darby, deceased. Dated 10 mo. 3, 1729, from Darby Mo. Mtg., Pa. Received 10 mo. 26, 1729. Not recorded.

JOSEPH ENGLAND, to marry ; dated 11 mo. 19, 1729, from Duck Creek Mo. Mtg., Delaware. Not recorded.

SARAH GATES, wife of Josiah Gates, coming over to live with her husband. Dated 11 mo. 21, 1729, from Poole Mo. Mtg., England. Received 3 mo. 25, 1733. Not recorded.

SAMUEL EMLY, returning, dated 1 mo. 16, 1729, from Two Weeks' Mtg. in London, England. Not recorded.

WILLIAM SANDWITH, unmarried, "who resided for some time in this City and is lately removed into your Parts." Dated 1 mo. 24, 1729–30, from Mtg. in Dublin, Ireland. Signed by Samuel Sandwith. Also a certificate dated 1 mo. 8, 1729, from Mtg. at Coledine, Ireland, where he has served his apprenticeship. He has now taken to seafaring. Original on file. Received 8 mo. 27, 1727.

ANN DUDLEY, unmarried; dated 11 mo. 19, 1729, from Mtg. at Bristol, England. Original on file. Received 2 mo. 24, 1730.

DINAH BUSHLY, unmarried; dated 3 mo. 6, 1729, from Dublin, Ireland. Original on file. Received 4 mo. 26, 1730.

EUNICE CONOLLY, unmarried, about to remove along with her mother and relatives and friends into Pennsylvania. She was not brought up as a Friend, but "hath lived as a Servant to Severall Friends of this city." Dated 6 mo. 12, 1729, from Mtg. at Dublin, Ireland. Original on file. Received 1 mo. 27, 1730.

MARY BONES, unmarried, "of Coverleys fields in ye Parish of Stepney." Dated 1 mo. 20, 1726–7, from Two Weeks' Mtg. in London, England. Also a certificate dated 9 mo. 13, 1727, for her from Bristol, England, where she has resided about six months. Original on file. Received at Philadelphia 1 mo. 7, 1730. Received 1 mo. 27, 1730.

HANNAH HUDSON, unmarried; dated 4 mo. 2, 1730, from Mtg. in Dublin, Ireland. Went to Pennsylvania about a year ago. Original on file.

RACHEL HEARON, unmarried; dated 4 mo. 10, 1723, from Mo. Mtg. at Newcastle, England. She has written from Pennsylvania for a certificate. Received 4 mo. 26, 1730.

JOHN SPARROW, unmarried, son of Anthony Sparrow, near Sudbury, co. of Suffolk, England, "having resided about seven years in London, in which time He has been convinced of truth." Dated 6 mo. 17, 1730, from Two Weeks' Mtg. at Devonshire House, London, England. Original on file. Received 10 mo. 25, 1730.

NATHANIEL JENKINS, of Bristol, cordwainer, and wife, dated 12 mo. 15, 1730–1, from Mtg. in Bristol, England. Original on file. Received 5 mo. 30, 1731.

WILLIAM NICHOLSON, unmarried, of Dublin, Ireland, dated 1 mo. 9, 1730–1. He was brought up as a friend by his uncle, Joseph Nicholson, of Dublin, "unto whom he was bound an apprentice but before his time was out his Unckle died and being inclinable to go to America, his Aunt who was his Mistress consented thereto and paid his Passage." Certificate from Dublin Mtg. Original on file. Received 7 mo. 29, 1732.

JOHN HILLBORNE, to marry Rachel Strickland, daughter of Miles Strickland, a member of Phila. Mtg. Dated 2 mo. 7, 1730, from Wrightstown Mo. Mtg., Bucks Co., Pa. At Phila., 1 mo. 27, 1730. Not recorded.

JOHN OXLEY, coming on business; dated 2 mo. 29, 1730, from Quarterly Mtg. in Barbadoes. Received 7 mo. 25, 1730. Not recorded.

EMME EVANS, dated 8 mo. 7, 1730, from Mo. Mtg. at Perquimans, North Carolina. Also one from Nansemond, Virginia, dated 8 mo. 27, 1730. Another from near Curles Mo. Mtg., Henrico Co., Va., dated 9 mo. 7, 1730. Received 11 mo. 29, 1730. Not recorded.

MARY JERVIS, dated 9 mo. 9, 1730, from Burlington Mo. Mtg., N. J. Received 5 mo. 30, 1731. Not recorded.

ALICE PAXSON, dated 10 mo. 28, 1730, from Abington Mo. Mtg., Pa. Received 2 mo. 30, 1731. Not recorded.

JOHN DILLWYN, about to return to Phila.; dated 11 mo. 6, 1730, from Mo. Mtg. at Horsleydown in Southwark, England. Not recorded.

ISABEL DANIEL, unmarried; dated 11 mo. 25, 1730–1, from Salem Mo. Mtg., N. J. Received 12 mo. 26, 1730. Not recorded.

ANN EVANS, dated 11 mo. 25, 1730–31, from Chester Mo. Mtg., Pa. Received 11 mo. 29, 1730. Not recorded.

HANNAH BALDWIN, unmarried; dated 11 mo. 25, 1730–31, from Chester Mo. Mtg., Pa. Not recorded.

MARY SHUTE, daughter of Thomas Shute, of Melksham, co. of Wilts, England, tallow-chandler; dated 1 mo, 6, 1731. Received 7 mo. 29, 1732. Not recorded.

ARMIEJER AND THOMAS TROTTER, unmarried; dated 1 mo. 11, 1730–1, from Mo. Mtg. at Chuckertuck, Virginia. Received 5 mo. 30, 1731. Not recorded.

CHARLES NORRIS, returning, dated 1 mo. 18, 1730–1, from Mo. Mtg. at Bridgetown, Barbadoes. Received 3 mo. 28, 1731. Not recorded.

STEPHEN PAYTON, dated 5 mo. 19, 1731, from Mo. Mtg. at Dudley, co. of Worcester, England. "About a year & half ago [he] acquainted us of his Intentions of going a trading voyage to the Plantations in America & requesting a Certificate from us * * * which we accordingly gave him since which having made the same voyage He has brought a Certificate with him from the Monthly Meeting held at Flushing on Long island ye 5th 9 mo., 1730." Now he signifies "his Intention of making another Voyage that way on a trading account." He has had "his residence amongst us for about three months." Certificate signed by Henry and John Payton. Original on file. Received 9 mo. 26, 1731.

JOHN STANES, unmarried, now in Pennsylvania. Dated 1 mo. 1, 1730–1, from Two Weeks' Meeting at Devonshire House, London, England. He was "too unadvisedly involved in a law suit," and the disadvantage "sustained thereby we Suppose was the occasion of his Removall." Original on file. Received 5 mo. 30, 1731.

JOHN KINSEY and wife, now in Pennsylvania. Dated 11 mo. 21, 1730, from Mo. Mtg. in Woodbridge. Original on file.

BENJAMIN LAY, a minister, and wife Sarah, dated 12 mo. 4, 1731, from Colchester Mo. Mtg. Original on file. Received 5 mo. 28, 1732.

LAWRENCE GROWDEN, unmarried, dated 12 mo. 14, 1731, from Meeting in City of Bristol, England. Original on file. Received 6 mo. 25, 1732.

SAMUEL FLOYD, unmarried, dated 4 mo.

30, 1732, from Meeting in Barbadoes. He comes to Pennsylvania "upon ye acctt. of Trade." Original on file. Received 6 mo. 25, 1732.

SAMUEL SANSOM, unmarried, dated 6 mo. 14, 1732, from Two Weeks Meeting at Devonshire House, London, England. Certificate signed by John Sansom. Original on file. Received 11 mo. 26, 1732.

EDWARD WALBANK, and wife. Dated 2 mo. 12, 1732, from Mo. Mtg. at Bull and Mouth, at the Chamber in Grace Church Street, London, England. "They came to live in this city [London] about the year 1715." Original on file. Received 6 mo. 25.

THOMAS PENN, unmarried, dated 3 mo. 8, 1732, from Two Weeks Meeting in London, England. "So desiring his Preservation and Wellfare that He may possess the Virtue of his Worthy Father whose memory is still dear unto us." Original on file. Received 6 mo. 25, 1732.

ELIZABETH HAWKINS, unmarried, dated 2 mo. 6, 1731, from Dublin, Ireland. Received 5 mo. 30, 1731. Not recorded.

SARAH SMITH, unmarried, dated 11 mo. 25, 1731, from Dublin, Ireland. Received 4 mo. 30, 1732. Not recorded.

BENJAMIN TOMLINSON, and wife, Mary, "having Removed themselves about Four years since unto your parts, & of Late by Letter Requested a Certificate from us to you." Dated 12 mo. 28, 1732, from Mo. Mtg. at Horsleydown, England. Received 6 mo. 31, 1733. Not recorded.

RUTH STEER, Jr., unmarried, "descended from an honest Parentage." Dated 3 mo. 23, 1734, from Six Weeks Mtg. at Lisburn, in the north of Ireland. Signed by Ruth Steere, Sr., Isaac, Catharine, Mary and Richard Steere. Received 2 mo. 26, 1735. Not recorded.

THOMAS CHALKLEY, "commander of the Barbadoes Pacquet, Sometime ago arrived at this Port from Phyladelphia and now Intending Shortly to return, Desired a few Lines from us by way of Certificate." Dated 6 mo. 20, 1734, from Dublin, Ireland. Not recorded.

JOHN MILLER, "A Stay Maker," with son and daughter; dated 8 mo. 4, 1732, from Mo. Mtg. at Westminster in the Savoy, London, England. Original on file.

JOHN RICHARDSON, unmarried, who resided "for Some years" in Pennsylvania; then "returned into this his Native Country & for a few years hath resided hereway at times within the compass of this monthly meeting." Dated 6 mo. 21, 1733. Original on file. Received 12 mo. 22, 1733-4.

GILES BRIMBLE, unmarried, now in Philadelphia; dated 7 mo. 24, 1733, from Meeting in Bristol. Original on file. Received 8 mo. 25, 1734.

PAULUS KRIPNER (certificate undated and name of meeting not given), "who sometime since went from Holland into your parts hath acquainted the meeting for sufferings that since his arrivall amongst you Some had misrepresented him as if he had carried with him the Money and books belonging to the Monthly Meeting of Amsterdam, and we being appointed by the Meeting for Suffering to lett you know the true State of the affair do hereby acquaint you that he having putt the said Mony & books into the hands of one Anthony Noble of Amsterdam and taken a Note promising to deliver the same to the sd Meetings order wch Note he sent to the Meeting accordingly, and we by order thereof Endorst and sent the same to Peter Leenders in Holland who hath acquainted us that the Books & mony has been recd. by him & two frds. more of Amsterdam for the Meetings use. And as to the life & conversation of the sd Paulus Kripner, we have heard He was first convinced of the Truth at the Cape of good Hope and afterward came to live in Amsterdam and had a great Contest with some who profess Truth there & yet use the ceremony of the Hatt & as this difference run very high, its not probable they would give him a Certificate. We have not heard him charged with any bad conversation in his dealings or otherwise." There are only three signers to the certificate: Simeon Warner, Richard How and Jacob Hagen. Original on file. Received at Phila., 7 mo. 27, 1734.

JOSEPH SAUNDERS, unmarried, nephew of Richard Saunders, "is lately gone on Shipboard * * * intending for Pensilvania." Dated 12 mo. 12, 1732, from Two Weeks Meeting at Bull and Mouth, London, England. Original on file. Received 4 mo. 28, 1734.

PATRICK OGILLSBY, who "hath been a resident among us for severall years." Dated 6 mo. 28, 1734, from Mo. Mtg. at Westbury, Long Island. Received 9 mo. 29, 1734.

ANN PENLY, daughter of John Penly, and Mary, his wife, both deceased. Dated 11 mo. 9, 1734–5, from Mo. Mtg. at Cirencester, co. of Gloucester. Original on file. Not recorded. Received 4 mo. 27, 1735.

PATRICK OGILLSBY, unmarried, dated 12 mo. 26, 1734–5, from Mo. Mtg. at Westbury, Long Island. Received 9 mo. 29, 1734. Not recorded.

RACHEL ALLEN, unmarried, "for Some time hath lived as a Servant in these parts * * * Intending to remove into your parts (with her Brother and Sister Joseph and Ann Unthank)." Dated 2 mo. 1, 1735, from Mo. Mtg. at Scarborough, co. of York, England. Received 8 mo. 31, 1735. Not recorded.

THOMAS WILLIAMS, "formerly a member of our said meeting and Mary his wife & divers Children. Children Removed from hence & Settled in Phyladelphia aforesaid, and where the said Thomas Williams is (as we are Informed) Since Dead, and hath left a poor Widdow and Several Helpless Children." Dated 9 mo. 19, 1735, from Mo. Mtg. held in Austle. Not recorded.

STEPHEN PAYTON, of Dudley, co. of Worcester, England, "being on a Trading Voyage for America." Dated 12 mo. 16, 1735, from Mo. Mtg. at Stonesbridge, co. of Worcester, England. Received 9 mo. 26, 1731. Not recorded.

ISAIAH MCNIECE, "who hath lived within the compass of our meeting these Twenty years." He is about to " remove from hence with some of his Children (he being a Widower) to Pensylvania." Dated 2 mo. 21, 1736, from Mtg. at Copte Hill, co. of Cavan, Ireland. Original on file. Received 7 mo. 24, 1736.

DAVID CLARKE, unmarried, son of John and Mary Clarke, late of Nailsworth, co. of Gloucester, England, deceased. Dated 2 mo.

10, 1735, from Mo. Mtg. at Paynswick, co. of Gloucester. Original on file. Received 7 mo. 24, 1736.

JOHN PATERSON, "who went from hence severall years ago & Since has resided in your parts is now about to marry a young woman amongst you and requesting a few lines from us by way of Certificate." He served his apprenticeship with a Friend of Dublin. Dated 3 mo. 25, 1736, from Mtg. in Dublin, Ireland. Original on file. Received 8 mo. 29, 1736.

DOCTOR SAMUEL CHEW and wife, Mary, now settled in Philadelphia. Dated 4 mo. 9, 1732, from Mo. Mtg. at the Cliffs, Western Shore, Md. Original on file. Received 5 mo. 30, 1736.

SAMUEL WALKER, unmarried, dated 4 mo. 6, 1735, from Mo. Mtg. of Richmond, held at Chantrey, Yorkshire, England. Original on file. Received 10 mo. 31, 1736.

ROBERT STRETTLE, wife and family. Children Amos, Frances and Ann are unmarried. Dated 11 mo. 26, 1736, from Mo. Mtg. at Horslydown, in Southwark, England. Original on file. Received 4 mo. 24, 1737.

JOHN GLENNY, unmarried; dated 3 mo. 4, 1736, from Mo. Mtg. at Henly upon Thomas, for the upper side of the county of Oxon, England. "When He came to Settle in our Parts he brought with him a Satisfactory certificate from North Brittaine by which we understand his Father was a friend and that He was Educated and brought up amongst them in the way of Truth." Original on file. Received 7 mo. 24, 1736.

JOHN BUSHELL, unmarried, dated 3 mo. 12, 1737, from Mo. Mtg. at Bridgetown, Barbadoes. Original on file. Received 4 mo. 24, 1737.

LEONARD SNOWDEN, unmarried, "the Bearer hereof who for severall years past has lived among us & taught School here having acquainted us that from the Good Encouragement thats given him for a Schoolmaster among you He is inclined to come into America & desires our Certificate." Dated 12 mo. 1, 1736–7, from Scarborough Mo. Mtg., held at Staintondale, Yorkshire, England. Original on file. Received 6 mo. 26, 1737.

LEWIS WESTON, unmarried, brother of Daniel Weston. Dated 12 mo. 7, 1736–7, from Two Weeks Mtg. at Bull and Mouth, London, England. Received 5 mo. 29, 1737.

JOHN FREEMAN and family, intending to remove to America; dated 11 mo. 29, 1735, from Mo. Mtg. at Lankford. Original on file.

WILLIAM BENNETT, unmarried, "late of Collum Stork," co. of Devon, "now in the

Province of Pensylvania." Dated 5 mo. 25, 1736. Original on file.

JOHN LUKE, unmarried, son of Jacob Luke, "sometime left this Island for your City." Dated 8 mo. 19, 1738, from Mo. Mtg. at Bridgetown, Barbadoes. Original on file. Received 11 mo. 26, 1738.

JAMES HILL and "wife Margaret Hill, alias Oliver." Dated 5 mo. 21, 1728, from Preparative Mtg. held near Balanderry, Ireland. Original on file. Received 10 mo. 29, 1738 ["they being lately removed to settle at Willingstown in New Castle County."]

BENJAMIN CALLENDER, unmarried, coming to the Province "on account of Trade." Dated 1 mo. 7, 1737–8, from Mo. Mtg. at Bridgetown, Barbadoes. Original on file. Received 2 mo. 28, 1738.

ELIZABETH DEANE, unmarried, dated 2 mo. 10, 1736, from Mtg. at Bellnacree, co. of Antrim, Ireland. Received 6 mo. 28, 1736. Not recorded.

WILLIAM CALLENDER, returning; dated 3 mo. 2, 1736, from Mo. Mtg. at Heathcot's Bay, Barbadoes. Received 4 mo. 29, 1733. Not recorded.

JOHN ARMITT, returning; dated 3 mo. 17, 1736, from Two Weeks Mtg. at Devonshire House, London, England. Not recorded.

MARTHA WALKER and daughter, Rebecca Walker, dated 1 mo. 3, 1737–8, from Mo. Mtg. at Richmond, Yorkshire, England. Received 6 mo. 25, 1738. Not recorded.

SARAH WILCOCKS, wife of Issachar Wilcocks, "some years ago remov'd with her sd. Husband into the Compass of your meeting." She was "marry'd by a priest to her present Husband." Dated 1 mo. 27, 1737, from Mo. Mtg. at Mountrath, Ireland. Received 11 mo. 27, 1737. Not recorded.

JOSEPH MARSHALL, unmarried, from Mansfield, England, dated 5 mo. 25, 1737. Also a letter dated Mansfield, July 25, 1737, from his parents, Ralph and Mary Marshall, confirming his letter of April 24, 1737, but expressing surprise "yt you are now turn'd Quaker." On the other side of the sheet is a letter dated Mansfield, July 25, 1737, from Mrs. Christ: Hopewell to her son Nathaniel. She mentions her son Joseph, has "sent 3 letters to you and has received but one I sent Some Receipts for making Ginger bread and buns in one of them." "Your Sister Betty is at Down lying on her seventh Child." Among the signatures on this MS. the original of which is on file, are those of Robert and Daniel Hopewell. Not recorded.

ELIZABETH MIFFLIN, lately married, dated

9 mo. 10, 1737, from Mo. Mtg. at Boston, Mass. Received 10 mo. 30, 1737. Not recorded.

MARY SHARP, about to remove, "in order to Live with her Husband James Sharp, who some time past left this City, and as we are Informed is Settled amongst you." Dated 1 mo. 28, 1738, from Dublin, Ireland. Not recorded.

RUTH WEBB, dated 1 mo. 31, 1736, from Mtg. in Lurgan, Ireland. She and Moses Shaw went "away from this place." Original on file. Received at Phila., 10 mo., 1736.

PAUL CHANDERS and family, removed sometime ago to Pennsylvania. Dated 7 mo. 19, 1738, from Mo. Mtg. at Hartshaw, Lancashire, England. Original on file.

BENJAMIN CALLENDER, unmarried, dated 3 mo, 17, 1739, from Mo. Mtg. at Bridgetown, Barbadoes. He comes on a trading voyage to Philadelphia. Original on file.

THOMAS ROOKE, unmarried, "Granson to our Ancient and Esteemed Friend George Rook of this City." Dated 1 mo. 12. 1739–40. from Mtg. in Dublin, Ireland.

JOSEPH SAUNDERS, unmarried, returning to Pennsylvania. Dated 1 mo. 8, 1735–6. Original on file. Received 4 mo. 28, 1734.

RACHEL SPENCE, unmarried, "haveing lived for some time Servant at Manchester within the compass of this Monthly Meeting." Dated 5 mo. 18, 1738, from Mo. Mtg. at Warrington, Lancashire, England. Received 12 mo. 24, 1738-9. Not recorded.

JANE SHALLEY, "hath acquainted us of her husbands intention to move her and the rest of his family to Pensylvania * * * ye Said Jane Shalley hath dwelt in this town near three years. She received friends principles Since She Came amongst us." Dated 6 mo. 9, 1739, from Mo. Mtg. at Boston, Mass. Received 7 mo. 29, 1739. Not recorded.

HUGH CANADY and family. The "Said Hugh frequainted our Religious meeting for worship from his Childhood, & Since his Wifes Decease (they being Maried orderly amongst us) has been Endusterous in Labouring for a livelihood for his Children, & Some of them being Grown up has behaved prity orderly Considering their yeares." Dated 2 mo. 3, 1741, from Men's Meeting held near Charlemount, Ireland. Original on file. Not recorded.

JOHN AMBLER, unmarried, son of Joseph Ambler, of Selby, co. of York, England. He intends to "Remove himself in order to Settle in Some Business in your parts." "He hath lived with his Father reputably in his Fathers business of Shopkeeping and is well Qualified as a Scholar to practice keeping a School for the Languages & for Writeing & Accompts." Dated 2 mo. 30, 1736, from Mo. Mtg. at Selby, Yorkshire. Original on file. Received 10 mo. 26, 1740.

JOSEPH SAUL, unmarried, "a young man who hath Lived and served his Apprenticeship to a Wheelmaker within the Compass of our Monthly Meeting." Dated 11 mo. 20, 1740-1, from Mo. Mtg. at Pardshaw Hall, Cumberland, England. Certificate signed by Anthony Saul. Original on file. Received 3 mo. 22, 1741.

ABEL CHAMBERLAIN, unmarried, dated 11 mo. 26, 1740, from Three Weeks Mtg. in Cork, Ireland. Original on file. Received 3 mo. 22, 1741.

JAMES MOORE, widower, dated 1 mo. 6, 1740-1, from Mtg. at Waterford, Ireland. Original on file. Received 4 mo. 26, 1741.

ISAAC WHITELOCK, dated 12 mo. 18, 1740-1, from Brighouse Mo. Mtg. held at Leeds, England. He returns to Pennsylvania. Original on file. Received 5 mo. 31, 1741.

JOSEPH DEANE, unmarried, son of Alexander Deane, "who formerly resided within the Compass of this Meeting & has lately left this in order to Transport himself to your Province he having been in sd Province before." Received 7 mo. 25, 1741.

JOSEPH STILES, son of Benjamin and Lucy Stiles, (the mother, deceased) of Newbury, co. of Berks, England. While young he "chose a Seafaring life" and has been "divers times in Philadelphia." Dated 5 mo. 21, 1741. Certificate signed by Henry Stiles. Original on file. Received 10 mo. 25, 1741.

JOHN ROBINS, unmarried, lately removed into Pennsylvania. Dated 3 mo. 25, 1741, from Two Weeks Mtg. in London, England. Original on file. Received 9 mo. 27, 1741.

JOSEPH GARNETT, unmarried, of Dublin, Ireland, dated 5 mo. 27, 1742, from Dublin Mtg. Original on file. At the Mo. Mtg., 10 mo. 31, 1742, he is reported to have returned to his home in Dublin.

ELIZABETH JOHNSON, unmarried, "on the Encouragement & Invitation of her Brother Ralph Loftus of Philadelphia removed from this place about ten months since with Intention to settle with you." Dated 3 mo. 10, 1742, from Mo. Mtg. at Sunderland, co. of Durham, England. Received 8 mo. 28, 1742. Not recorded.

JOHN OXLEY, about to take a voyage to Pennsylvania for his health. Dated 2 mo. 7, 1743. Not recorded.

THOMAS ROBINSON, unmarried, of Dublin, dated 2 mo. 11, 1738, from Mtg. in Dublin, Ireland. Original on file. Not recorded. At Phila., 6 mo. 31, 1739.

JOHN BRINGHURST, Jr., returning to his native land, 7 mo. 20, 1744, from Mo. Mtg. at Bridgetown, Barbadoes. Not recorded.

SAMUEL SHOEMAKER, returning, dated 5 mo. 29, 1745, from London, England. Not recorded.

GEORGE MIFFLIN, returning, dated 5 mo. 29, 1745, from London, England. Not recorded.

JOEL NEAVE, unmarried; dated 7 mo. 27, 1742, from Two Weeks Mtg. in London, England. Original on file. Received 11 mo. 28, 1742.

JESSE BOURNE, unmarried, "of Cheapside Citizen and Glover of London Son of Benjamin Bourne of London Citizen & Glover," intending to make a voyage to Pennsylvania "on account of Trade." Dated 12 mo. 14, 1742, from Two Weeks Mtg. at Grace Church Street, London, England. Original on file. Received 4 mo. 24, 1743.

JOHN BODY, unmarried, dated 6 mo. 5, 1743, from Mo. Mtg. at Richmond, held at Swinnithwait, Yorkshire, England. Original on file. Received 12 mo. 24, 1743.

JOHN SHAW, wife and family. Dated 6 mo. 6, 1745, from Mo. Mtg. at Maidenhead, co. of Berks, England. Original on file.

FRANCIS NASH, unmarried, dated 5 mo. 10, 1746, from Mo. Mtg. at Leominster. Original on file. Received 10 mo. 26, 1746.

SAMUEL BRYAN, unmarried, returning to Pennsylvania. Dated 6 mo. 11, 1746, from London, England. Original on file. Received 8 mo. 29, 1742.

WILLIAM DICKENSON, unmarried, dated 6 mo. 14, 1746, from Pontefroct Mo. Mtg. held at Lanehead, Yorkshire, England. Signed by Elihu Dickenson, Clerk, Samuel Dickenson, and Elizabeth Dickenson. Original on file.

WILLIAM GRIFFITTS, unmarried, dated 5 mo. 19, 1746, from Mtg. at Swanzey. Original on file. Received 10 mo. 26, 1746.

JOSHUA CROSBY, and nephew THOMAS CROSBY, both unmarried, "late of this Island but now in Philadelphia." Dated Feb. 9, 1746, from Jamaica. Original on file. At Phila., 6 mo. 29, 1746.

JOHN HAYDOCK, unmarried, son of Robert Haydock, "late from England but last from your parts." Dated 3 mo. 7, 1747, from Mo. Mtg. at Flushing, Long Island. Received 8 mo. 30, 1747.

JONAS LANGFORD REDWOOD, son of Abraham Redwood, whose father places him in Philadelphia for a few years. Dated 7 mo. 29, 1747, from Mo. Mtg. at Newport, Rhode Island. Original on file. Received 9 mo. 27, 1747.

MEHITABLE REDWOOD, whose father, Abraham Redwood, "required her to Reside amongst you for some time" for her improvement. Dated 7 mo. 29, 1747, from Mo. Mtg. at Newport, Rhode Island. Original on file. Received 8 mo. 30, 1747.

DAVID DEAN, "a young man who was born and hitherto Educated within the bounds of this Meeting." Unmarried. Dated 2 mo. 25, 1747, from Mtg. in Antrim, Ireland. Received 10 mo. 25, 1747.

DR. ROBERT WILLAN, unmarried, dated 12 mo. 2, 1747–8, from Mo. Mtg. of Scarborough, held at Staintondale, Yorkshire, England, "in order to undertake the keeping Friends' School." Received 6 mo. 26, 1748.

JOHN WILLIAMSON, unmarried, blacksmith and farrier, a birthright member, dated 3 mo. 24, 1748, from Pardshaw Mo. Mtg., England. Original on file. Received 9 mo. 25, 1748.

BENJAMIN BAGNELL, Jr., and wife Ann, "lately removed" to Philadelphia. Dated 6 mo. 11, 1748, from Mo. Mtg. at Boston, Mass.

Signed by Benjamin and Sarah Bagnell. Original on file. Received 12 mo. 24, 1748.

MARTHA PETEL "removed from us about Six years past Since which we understand She has Resided in or near your City." Dated 10 mo. 12, 1745, from Mo. Mtg. at Lynn, Mass. Received 1 mo. 25, 1748. Not recorded.

REBECCA WARDELL, "who moved from Boston to your City with her Husband has desired of us a few lines by way of Certificate." Dated 5 mo. 11, 1745, from Mo. Mtg. at Salem, New England. Received 7 mo. 21, 1745. Not recorded.

ROBERT STRETTELL, unmarried, the younger, being about to remove hence to your city. Dated 1 mo. 18, 1745–6, from Dublin, Ireland. Original on file. Not recorded. Signed by Thomas Strettell, Jr.

SOPHIA HUME, widow, has resided "for some time in this City & hath acquainted us by her Letter that She was for returning to South Carolina." Dated 7 mo. 2, 1747, from Mo. Mtg. at Devonshire House, London, England. Received 5 mo. 29, 1748. Not recorded.

JOHN LUKE, "having been very sickly for some time past & on that account designing to take a Voyage, in hopes of recovering his Health." Date d 3 mo. 11, 1749, from Mo.

Mtg. in Bridgetown, Barbadoes. Received 10 mo. 29, 1749. Not recorded.

SAMUEL BURGE, unmarried, dated 5 mo. 24, 1749, from Two Weeks Mtg. at Grace Church Street, London, England. Not recorded.

JAMES PEMBERTON, returning, dated 5 mo. 24, 1749, from London, England. Not recorded.

CHARLES NORRIS, about to return; dated 7 mo. 18, 1749, from Mtg. at Grace Church Street, London, England. Not recorded.

JOSEPH PARKER, unmarried, dated 8 mo. 30, 1749, from Mtg. at Grace Church St., London, England. Received 1 mo. 29, 1745. Not recorded.

JOHN DAVIS, about to remove; dated 12 mo. 19, 1749, from Mtg. at Grace Church Street, London, England. Received 3 mo. 26, 1749. Not recorded.

PATIENCE RICHARDSON, unmarried, dated 6 mo. 28, 1750, from Dublin, Ireland. Original on file. Recorded. Received 12 mo. 27, 1751.

SARAH HIDE, daughter of Edmund and Sarah Hide, having removed herself into Pennsylvania. Dated 6 mo. 12, 1748, from

Two Weeks Mtg., in London, England. Original on file. Received 4 mo. 30, 1749.

JOHN DAVIS, unmarried, dated 12 mo. 8, 1748, from Mo. Mtg. at Horsleydown, in Southwark, England. Original on file. Received 3 mo. 26, 1749.

ELIZABETH GRIDLY, "who has resided for some years a Servant in the Family of Thomas & Elizabeth Gray of Godmanchester." She intends "to remove from hence to her Unckle Samuel Gridley resident within the Compass of your said Monthly Meeting." Dated 6 mo. 1, 1749, from Mo. Mtg. at Ives, co. of Huntingdon, England. Original on file.

JAMES WAGSTAFF, a member of Peel Mo. Mtg., now in Pa., brother of Thomas Wagstaff. Dated 1 mo. 19, 1749, from Two Weeks Mtg. in London. Signed by William, Thomas, and John Wagstaffe. Original on file.

SARAH KNUBLEY, [Knably] daughter of John Knubley, of Skinberness, deceased. Certificate addressed to William and Jane Hinton, at Philadelphia, recommending "her to you in order that you might not doubt the certainty of her being your brothers daughter." She has "been at service for sometime, and likewise of late she have come amongst friends." From Particular Meeting at "Beckfoot Foull Wath in the Lordship of Abby Holm in the

County of Cumberland in Old England this 29th of 10 mo., 1744." Original on file. Received 2 mo. 26, 1745.

MARY GLADING, daughter of Richard and Ann Glading, " having removed herself from hence in the station of a Servant to Gervas Burgess a Friend of Your Country." Dated 1 mo. 5, 1749, from Mo. Mtg. held in Hertford, England. Original on file. Received 7 mo. 28, 1750.

WILLIAM NICHOLLS, dated 12 mo. 8, 1748, from Mo. Mtg. in Horseleydown, in Southwark, England. Original on file. Received 9 mo. 30, 1750.

WILLIAM SHIPLEY, Jr., wife, and child; dated 2 mo. 26, 1750, from Mo. Mtg. at Stafford, England. Signed by John and Joseph Shipley. Original on file. Received 10 mo. 28, 1750.

JOHN BRITTEN, wife and family. Children: Jacob, John, and Susanna are unmarried. Dated 2 mo. 8, 1750, from Mtg. at Cooledine, co. of Wexford, Ireland. Original on file. Received 6 mo. 31, 1750.

THOMAS DAVIS, dated 12 mo. 5, 1750, from Dacer, Westmoreland, England. " He was not Joynd in Society with us when in this Country." Original on file. Received 5 mo. 26, 1751.

AUGUSTINE MELLER, dated 12 mo. 28, 1750, from Mo. Mtg. near Spightstown, Barbadoes. Original on file.

JOHN NEVITT, "having a mind to accompany his Brother into your parts & to return to us again." Dated 2 mo. 28, 1751, from Mo. Mtg. at the Moat, Ireland. Received 8 mo. 25, 1751.

JOHN TAGART and wife, Mary; dated 5 mo. 11, 1750, from Mtg. in Lurgan, Ireland. Original on file.

REBECCA RICHARDSON, widow of Zachary Richardson, and daughter, Elizabeth Clark, "about to return back to Pensilvania." Dated 8 mo. 6, 1746, from Mo. Mtg. at Horseleydown, Southwark, England. Original on file.

MARY ERWIN, going with her husband, John Erwin. Dated 4 mo. 19, 1739, from Mtg. at Dublin, Ireland. Original on file. Received 12 mo. 31, 1756.

ELIZABETH LITTLE, unmarried, "Some time agoe removed from this City to Settle in Pensilvania." She was "for Some time a servant in this City." Dated 1 mo. 12, 1750–1, from Dublin, Ireland.

JOHN WILLSON, schoolmaster, unmarried; dated 6 mo. 30, 1750, from Mo. Mtg. at Ackworth, England. Original on file. Received 10 mo. 28, 1750, he being "now usher of Friends School in this City."

JOSEPH MICKLE, going to America on business ; dated 4 mo. 5, 1750, from Mtg. at Dublin, Ireland. Original on file. Received 2 mo. 26, 1751.

JOHN WYLEY, going to America on business ; dated 4 mo. 5, 1750, from Mtg. at Dublin, Ireland. Original on file. Received 2 mo. 26, 1751.

DAVID BEAVIRGE, "having with Consent of his Parents removed himself from this city to London for the better encouragement in his business, but not finding matters there answer his expectations, Has thought fitt to try his fortune at Philadelphia where He now is." He served his master " three years preceeding the term of Whitsunday last in the Mercerway." Dated 11 mo. 31, 1750–1, from Mo. Mtg. at Edinburgh. Original on file. Received 5 mo. 26, 1751.

INDEX.

INDEX.

INDEX.

INDEX.

(126)

INDEX.

INDEX.

INDEX.

INDEX.

www.ingramcontent.com/pod-product-compliance
Lightning Source LLC
Chambersburg PA
CBHW030252030426
42336CB00009B/361